DR RANJ
BRAIN
POWER

A TOOLKIT TO UNDERSTAND AND TRAIN YOUR UNIQUE BRAIN

Illustrated by
DAVID O'CONNELL

First published in Great Britain in 2022 by Wren & Rook

ISBN: 978 1 5263 6297 1
E-book ISBN: 978 1 5263 6296 4

1 3 5 7 9 10 8 6 4 2

Alexa ® is a registered trademark of Amazon Europe Core S.à r.l. Siri ® is a registered
trademark of Apple Inc. Google Assistant ® is a registered trademark of Google LLC. Teflon®
is a registered trademark of The Chemours Company FC, LLC. Pokémon ® is a registered
trademark of Nintendo Co., Ltd. Grammy ® is a registered trademark of National Academy
of Recording Arts and Sciences, Inc. Oscar ® is a registered trademark of Academy of Motion
Picture Arts and Sciences. Strictly Come Dancing ® is a registered trademark of
The British Broadcasting Corporation. So You Think You Can Dance ® is a registered
trademark of 19 Entertainment Limited.

MIX
Paper from
responsible sources
FSC® C104740
www.fsc.org

Wren & Rook
An imprint of
Hachette Children's Group
Part of Hodder & Stoughton
Carmelite House
50 Victoria Embankment
London EC4Y 0DZ

An Hachette UK Company
www.hachette.co.uk
www.hachettechildrens.co.uk

Printed in China

The website addresses (URLs) included in this book were
valid at the time of going to press. However, it is possible that contents or addresses may
have changed since the publication of this book. No responsibility for any such changes can
be accepted by either the author or the publisher.

CONTENTS

BRAINS ARE BRILL!

Yes, they really are the bee's knees! Actually, brains and knees are very different parts of the body. And what do bees even have to do with anything, I hear you ask? Fair point. But trust me on this: brains are pretty cool.

~~~~~~~~~~~~~~~~~~~~

WHY ARE BRAINS SO COOL?

THINK ABOUT IT.

That's pretty funny in itself, because you're using your brain to think about your brain. And you're using your brain to read this book, which is telling you to think about your brain, using your brain ... Oh dear, my brain hurts. I could go on, but I'll stop before I confuse us both!

Your brain is actually quite incredible. Did you know it's made of around **100 BILLION** cells? If you lined up

100 billion peas all in a row, the line would go around the planet 25 times! Those cells also make it the most powerful supercomputer in the world, but it only uses a fraction of the energy needed to power a light bulb.

All that in a squishy lump of stuff sitting inside your head. That doesn't sound very cool, but its coolness lies in this: it is in charge of **ABSOLUTELY EVERYTHING** in your body. Things you see, hear, feel, smell and taste, as well as everything you do — including stuff you do without realising. While you've been reading this sentence, your brain has probably just told your mouth to swallow! There, you just did it, didn't you?

If we removed your brain, you would probably survive, but only doing the very basics. You'd be able to breathe and eat. However, you wouldn't be able to think about what you're going to do after school, or read your favourite stories, or play your favourite games, or feel like **YOU**. That's why your brain is so important. And it does all this 24 hours a day, 365 days a year. Amazing!

This also means that you have to look after it, because you can't replace it. Unlike some of the other organs in your body, you can't swap brains with anyone if it goes wrong. And we know that because people have tried!

In 1908, two doctors called Dr Alexis Carrel and Dr Charles Guthrie transplanted the head of one dog onto the neck of another. I know, proper Frankenstein stuff! Unfortunately, the 'Frankendog' experiment didn't work and sadly the dog died soon after. But people didn't learn their lesson there. In 1970, an American doctor called Dr Robert White tried a similar 'head swap' experiment with monkeys. Guess what? It didn't work out too well for the monkeys either. Poor monkeys.

That doesn't mean we'll never be able to transplant a brain from one person to another, but it's a long, long way off. So in the meantime, it's best just to look after the brain you have.

BRAINS HAVE FASCINATED US FOR THOUSANDS OF YEARS...

The ancient Egyptians used to think that all your thoughts came from your heart. So when someone died, they would carefully mummify that person's body (including their heart), preserving all the important bits. But,

oops — they sucked out the brain through a hole in the skull (**EWWWW**) and tossed it in the bin because they didn't think it was anything special. Awkward.

However, an old Egyptian piece of papyrus (that's like old-school paper) from 1700 BCE has details about the brain and nervous system, so some Egyptians must have realised its importance.

In 170 BCE, there was a Greek doctor called Galen who looked after all the Roman gladiators. He was one of the first people to say that your feelings and all the different functions of your body were controlled by your brain.

But it wasn't until 1543 that the first book about 'neuroscience' (which means studying the brain) was written, by a doctor from from what is now Belgium called Andreas Vesalius. He cut open dead bodies and had a look inside to see how they were put together. Most people would call that messy, but clever people call it **ANATOMY**. His book contained really detailed drawings and descriptions about the brain for the first time ever. He didn't get everything spot on though ... he also recommended removing people's blood from their bodies to cure their illnesses, which I do not recommend.

Luckily, we don't have to cut people up to learn about their brains any more. We now have really powerful scanners (called CT and MRI scanners) that let us see inside your head and all the different parts of the brain without you feeling a thing. They look like giant doughnuts, but you can't eat them I'm afraid. The technicians would get a bit annoyed, and they don't taste very nice!

While scientists have spent centuries obsessing over what your brain does and how it works, other people have been trying to figure out how we're able to think and have feelings — in other words, where our minds come from.

In 1649, a French philosopher called René Descartes came up with the idea that while your brain controls your body, your mind is something separate. Not literally separate. He didn't mean it was hanging out of the back of your head! But he meant separate in the sense that your mind seems to be bigger than your brain — your mind somehow takes up your whole being.

BRAINS ARE THE FUTURE...

All of these discoveries have taught us about how amazing your brain (and mind) are. So much so that scientists have been trying to recreate what the human brain does in machine form. Have you heard of something called artificial intelligence, or AI?

Imagine it's the 1940s during the Second World War, when the Nazis of Germany were fighting against lots of other countries. The Nazis would communicate secretly using a special code made by a machine called Enigma. However, an amazing British mathematician called Alan Turing invented a computer which cracked that code, and that breakthrough helped win the war. Yes, Alan Turing is probably the most **AWESOME** Alan in history.

He changed history a second time when he wrote about the possibility of creating machines that think like humans, and his initial insights eventually led to the creation of artificial intelligence — computers that 'think' a bit like human brains do. But your brain is more complex and much more powerful than the world's best supercomputer. No machine currently exists that can do everything your brain does. Artificial intelligence is getting more sophisticated every day though. If you've ever used Siri, Alexa or Google Assistant, then you've been using something that is based on artificial intelligence. Who knows what AI will be able to do in the future?

WHY AM I SO CLUED UP ABOUT BRAINS?

I've been a doctor for twenty years and that means I know a little about how the brain works and how to help when things don't quite go to plan. However, I started learning about the brain properly when I went to university. I even did a project where I spent a lot of time cutting up rats' brains. **YUCK!**

Now, as a doctor who treats children and young people, I look after people whose brains may be hurt or not working properly. I also care for people who are struggling with their mental health.

YOUR MENTAL WHAT?

We all know that being healthy and looking after your body is important. That's what we call physical health. But what about your mind? Well, looking after your brain and mind is just as important so that they can work correctly and we can live happy lives. That's what we mean by mental health. It's about how you feel and deal with all the things in the world.

I've had times when my own mental health hasn't been great and I got through it. It wasn't always easy, but I'm in a much better place now and I'm here to tell you all about it! I want you to remember that, however you feel or whatever is happening in your life, you're never alone and there is always someone to help if you are finding things tough.

WHY SHOULD YOU KEEP READING THIS BOOK?

So we're all agreed: brains are cool, yes? Great: my job's done, you can stop reading!

WAIT, COME BACK! I'm only joking.

It's important you agree that all brains are cool because we're going to spend a lot of the rest of the book talking about how **YOUR** specific brain is completely and utterly brilliant. Even though they all look similar, your brain is totally unique to you, just like your friend's brain is totally unique to them. Everyone's brain is a bit different, and works in its own special way to make them who they are. And brains are things of beauty to be proud of. So in this book, I want to show you just how incredible your brain is, how you can get to know it better and how you can help it be the best it can possibly be. That's right, we're going to **TRAIN YOUR BRAIN!**

I'll even let you into a little secret: once you understand your brain and mind, you'll figure out more about who you are — and how to get the most out of life. It'll help you feel supercharged with confidence. That's why this book is called **BRAIN POWER**. Because understanding your brain really can make you feel like a superhero.

BEFORE WE START . . .

Let's find out what you know (or think you know) already. See if you can tell whether these five brain-busting facts are true or false. You'll get the answers at the end of the book, but try not to sneak a peek!

1) Your brain is mainly made of water.

2) Messages to or from your brain travel at 100 kilometres per hour.

3) The animal with the biggest brain is the elephant.

4) Sleep is important because it's when your brain makes memories.

5) The left side of your brain controls the right side of your body (and vice versa).

Want to know the answers? Keep reading!

HOW TO
BUILD a
BRAIN

1

Your brain is responsible for everything you feel and do, and for making you, you. But how exactly does it do that?

If we're going to understand your brain properly, we'll need to learn how it's put together. We could try taking the top of your head off, scooping out your brain with a giant spoon and then laying it out flat on the table to get a really good look. But the mess would be awful. So I'll just have to tell you about it instead.

YOUR 'BRAINSTRUCTION' MANUAL

This chapter is going to be like a brain instruction manual — or a 'brainstruction' manual (see what I did there?). And we're going to be learning lots of technical stuff, so you'll need to think like a scientist.

To start, here's a picture of what your brain looks like. It has three main sections to it:

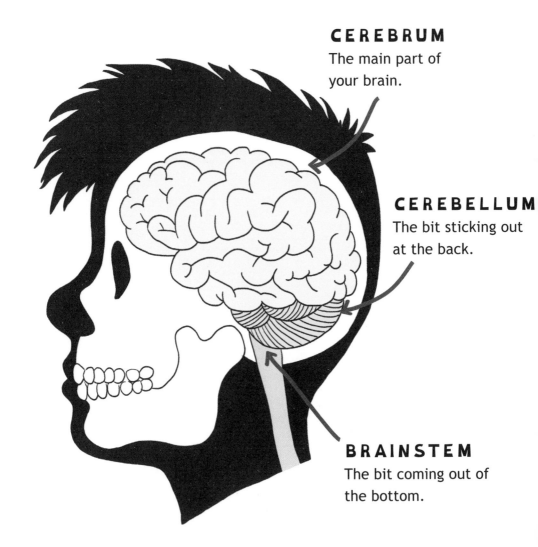

CEREBRUM
The main part of your brain.

CEREBELLUM
The bit sticking out at the back.

BRAINSTEM
The bit coming out of the bottom.

It kind of looks like a giant shrivelled-up prune inside your head. Why is it so wrinkly? Because it's folded up so you can fit as much brain as possible into a small space. If you unfolded and laid your brain out flat, it would be the size of a pillow (and be as flat as a pancake)! Some pictures of brains make them look pink, but the truth is that your brain is actually grey. It's also really squidgy because it's mainly made up of water, protein and fat — just like soup. But don't worry, your skull is not full of soup (though sometimes I do wonder about my brother's ...)!

Just like soup is made from lots of different ingredients, the food we eat contains all the ingredients our bodies need. This includes things like protein and fat, as well as the water we drink. All of these help make up the stuff inside our bodies, including our brains. Around three-quarters of your brain is made of water. So if you were to stop drinking for long enough, first you'd start to feel thirsty because your brain would tell you that you need to drink, and then eventually your brain would start to shrink and dry up! Unfortunately this would also mean it would stop working properly and you'd be really unwell. So do not try this at home! In fact, it's probably best just to listen to your parents and make sure you drink enough water, OK!? Please don't get me into trouble.

Your brain is cleverly organised into different parts.
Each one does a specific job. Let's take a closer look:

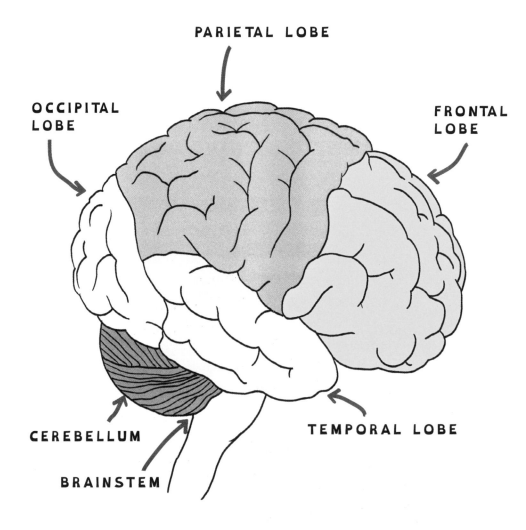

PARIETAL LOBE

OCCIPITAL
LOBE

FRONTAL
LOBE

CEREBELLUM

BRAINSTEM

TEMPORAL LOBE

FRONTAL LOBE

Where you do all your important thinking and decision-making. It also controls movement and speaking. That time you thought you were a superhero and decided it would be a good idea to jump from the fifth step, sprained your ankle and shouted OUCH! when you landed? You can thank your frontal lobe for all that.

PARIETAL LOBE

Where you experience the world around you, like when you touch something. So when you stub your toe on the corner of your desk and immediately jump up and down in pain, that's your parietal lobe kicking into action.

TEMPORAL LOBE

Deals with things like hearing, memory and emotions. Remember your favourite nursery rhyme from when you were a much smaller person? Well, that's sitting somewhere in here!

OCCIPITAL LOBE

In charge of what you see and uses information from your eyes to recognise objects and colours. It also helps you get an idea about how far away things are. You're using this part as you read this book right now.

CEREBELLUM

Helps control balance and movement. If you like dancing, you probably use this part of your brain quite a lot.

BRAINSTEM

Connects your brain to your spinal cord. The spinal cord is the bundle of nerves that comes out of the bottom of your skull and runs down your back. The brainstem also does things like makes sure you breathe, that your heart keeps beating, and other things that you probably don't pay attention to.

HOW DO WE KNOW WHAT DOES WHAT?

Unlike the diagrams you've just seen, brains don't come ready-labelled inside the body. It's only because of experiments throughout history that we've managed to work out what each bit does. For example, it was a doctor called John Martyn Harlow in the 1800s who worked out that your frontal lobe does all the clever stuff and helps create your personality.

He realised this when one of his patients had a horrible accident and an iron rod went through his head. The person eventually recovered but his frontal lobe was seriously damaged, and his behaviour changed. He went from being someone who was smart, level-headed and popular to someone who was immature, impatient and inconsiderate of others. It was like he was a different person, all because of an iron rod through the brain. I know what you're thinking: why does brain history have to be so gruesome all the time?!

Luckily, these days we can do special brain scans called PET or fMRI scans, which show us which bits of the brain are being used when we do certain things. No iron rods required — phew!

And sometimes, we don't even need a fancy machine. In 2020, a lady called Dagmar Turner had an operation on a brain tumour at King's College Hospital, London. Dagmar played the violin while the surgeons were operating on her brain tumour so they could make sure they didn't damage any parts of the brain that controlled her hand movements. How incredible is that?!

UNDER THE MICROSCOPE

Let's get really scientific now. Imagine you're looking at the brain through a powerful microscope. What would you see?

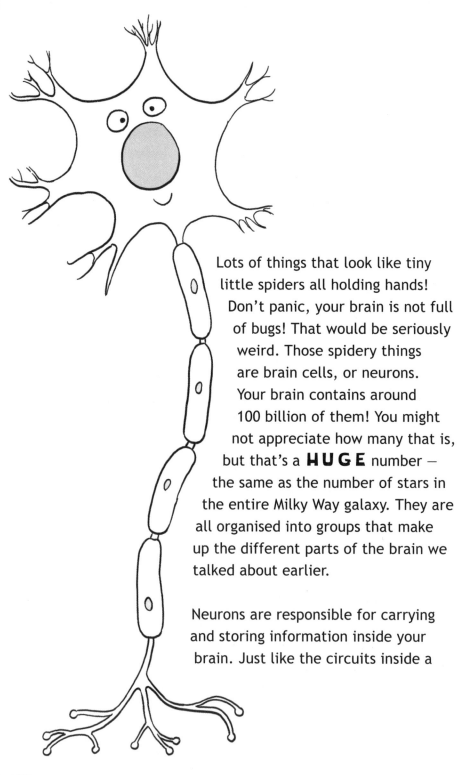

Lots of things that look like tiny little spiders all holding hands! Don't panic, your brain is not full of bugs! That would be seriously weird. Those spidery things are brain cells, or neurons. Your brain contains around 100 billion of them! You might not appreciate how many that is, but that's a **HUGE** number — the same as the number of stars in the entire Milky Way galaxy. They are all organised into groups that make up the different parts of the brain we talked about earlier.

Neurons are responsible for carrying and storing information inside your brain. Just like the circuits inside a computer, neurons connect with each other and make tiny circuits. And they carry that information using electricity too. Did you know that these electrical signals travel at over 400 kilometres per hour? That's faster than a Formula 1 racing car!

BACK TO THE BEGINNING

Now that we know what your brain looks like and what it's made up of, let's go back and explore how it all started. So cast your mind back to before you were a baby.

OK, that's impossible because you won't remember any of that. So let me fill you in ...

Your brain starts developing long before you are born, while you are an embryo (that's what we call you when you aren't yet born and are still really tiny — you've only been in the womb for three to four weeks at this point!). It starts off as a tiny tube, called the neural tube, which is a few millimetres long. This tube then grows and starts to fold up. Different parts of the tube go on to make different parts of the brain, and the last bit makes the spinal cord. So everything inside your head started off as a tiny straw!

STAGES OF BRAIN DEVELOPMENT IN AN EMBRYO

29 DAYS

33 DAYS

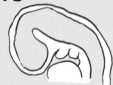

52 DAYS

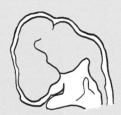

59 DAYS

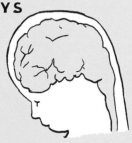

70 DAYS

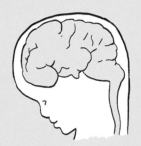

20 WEEKS

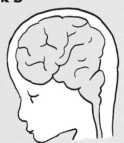

6 MONTHS

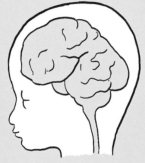

9 MONTHS

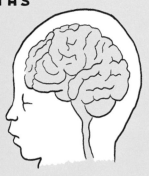

Fortunately, our brains don't stay that small and they grow rapidly to become what you have today.

YOU'RE THE 'BRAINY' ONE!

You may not have realised it, but you are. By the age of six, your brain is already almost as big as it will be when you're a fully grown adult. Now I understand why everyone told me I had such a big head when I was a kid. It must have been because my brain was **ENORMOUS!** At least, that's what I tell myself.

But it's not just about the size of your brain itself. The size of your brain compared to your body matters, as well as how developed it is. This is why humans are more clever than animals that are much bigger than us.

A sperm whale has the biggest brain of all among the animal kingdom, but it's not the most intelligent creature. That's partly because its brain is not as developed as ours is, but also because its brain is small compared to its body. And while humans are a lot smaller than whales, our brains are quite big in comparison to our bodies. Turn the page to see what I mean — a sperm whale's brain looks titchy when you see it inside its body. And are you surprised that a human brain is basically the same size as an elephant's?

CAT HUMAN ELEPHANT

SPERM WHALE

You may have heard some people say that we only use ten per cent of our brains. It's not true, but lots of people believe it. We know from brain scans that most of the brain is being used all the time — even when you are asleep.

However, there are many parts of the brain that do the same thing. This is what we call redundancy. We think our brains work this way just to make sure that if one bit stops working properly, another bit can take over. Always good to have a spare!

So the next time someone tells you to 'use your brain' — tell them that you are! Most of it!

ARE BOYS' AND GIRLS' BRAINS DIFFERENT?

We've all heard it before: boys are naturally better at things like sport, and girls are naturally better at art. And boys are noisy and rough while girls are gentle and quiet. Hmmm, sounds a bit fishy to me.

For many years we believed that boys and girls liked or were good at different things because their brains were really different. However, it's not as simple as that. Boys' and girls' brains are actually quite similar, but children's brains can change depending on what happens to them. So the things you see and do when you're young, the way you are brought up, and what you do at school and home can all change your brain while it is growing. It's quite likely that the reason boys and girls seem different is because they are always expected to do different things. For instance, boys have traditionally been encouraged to be more physical and sporty, whereas girls are often given more opportunities to do quieter activities like art. But it doesn't have to be that way!

Even though some people seem to be naturally good at certain things, we are all born with brains that are pretty much the same. As we grow up, our brains start to become unique to each of us based on how we choose to spend our time.

So girls, you are more than welcome to go out and play football. Go and climb mountains. Drive racing cars and become world leaders. Boys, feel free to dance. Design and make cool clothes for the world to wear. Be kind and caring to those around you.

WHATEVER YOU WANT TO DO, YOUR BRAIN IS READY TO BE AMAZING AT ANYTHING YOU SET YOUR MIND TO!

Don't believe me? Read on ...

YOU ARE BUILT
TO LEARN

One thing I've realised as an adult is that I used to learn things much more quickly when I was younger. And that's because children's brains are turbo-wired to learn faster than adults'. Right now, your brain is primed and ready to learn new skills better than any grown-up ever could!

Here's why ...

1)   Your brain is growing rapidly, and the neurons inside are making new connections faster than at any other time in life. Young brains are also more adaptable. That means they're able to change to do things better and faster.

2)   You don't have the same responsibilities that adults do (like earning money so you have somewhere to live), so your brain can use more of its power for learning cool new stuff. That's why so many grown-ups say that they would love to be children again, because they had less to worry about and could focus on the stuff they loved.

3)   Young people are braver and more keen to try new things out, so they learn fresh skills. Grown-ups are more likely to be worried about looking

silly and so decide to play it safe with what they already know.

4) Children tend to sleep for longer than adults, and we know that sleep is important for learning and making memories (more on this in chapter 5).

So if you want to learn a new language, to play an instrument, or find out how to do a hardflip on a skateboard, then now is the time! Just make sure you do it safely, OK? There are even ways we can **TRAIN** our **BRAINS** to get good at stuff — in chapter 4 we'll discover some brilliant brain-training exercises for you to try out.

BEWARE THE BUMPS

As amazing as your brain is, it cannot repair itself if it gets injured, unlike other parts of your body. For instance, if you fall and break your arm, it will heal because the bones in it repair themselves. However, if you have a bad fall and hurt your brain, your brain cells can't repair themselves so the damage could affect you for a long time. That's why it's so important to wear a helmet to protect your head when you're doing certain sports or activities like riding a bike, horse riding or mountain climbing.

If you do take a knock to the head and you feel unwell afterwards, always tell a grown-up straight away. You may have something called concussion. This is where the electrical activity in your brain cells becomes disturbed, so the cells need a bit of time to recover. Some people experience concussion as headaches. Others feel really groggy and find it hard to concentrate, or they might feel really anxious all the time. This needs to be taken seriously as you may need to see a doctor and take some time out to rest.

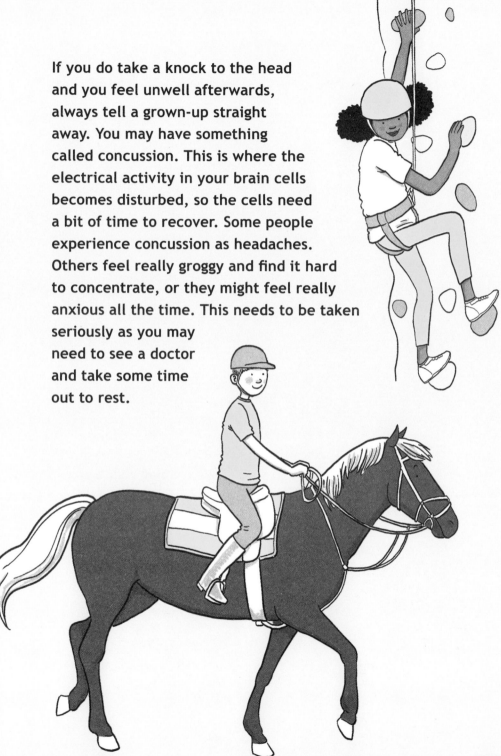

BRAINS GROW OLD TOO

Our brains may be fantastic, but sadly they are not immortal ... As we get older, our brains get older too. They might become a little bit slower (so you can't whizz around on your scooter like you used to). They may not be as organised as they once were (and you might be a little forgetful at times).

You may have noticed some of these things in your grandparents or the nice old neighbour who lives a few doors down. However, there are things that we can all do to try to keep our brains in tip-top condition for as long as possible:

1) **EXERCISE YOUR BRAIN** – keeping our brains active for as long as possible helps them stay fit (just like our bodies). So doing things like puzzles, brain games and reading will keep your brain going strong.

2) **BRAIN FOOD** – specific 'brain food' isn't a real thing, since no food can make you more clever, I'm afraid. However, trying to eat more healthy food and drinking enough water will keep your body and brain in good shape.

3) **BE FRIENDLY** – being nice and doing things with other people not only helps you feel

happier, but is actually good for your brain too. See, when your mum told you to be nice to other people, she had a point!

4) **GET SOME REST** – your brain needs rest at the end of a long day, just like your body does. So go to bed when your parents tell you to!

There are more tips on looking after your brain in the chapters coming up.

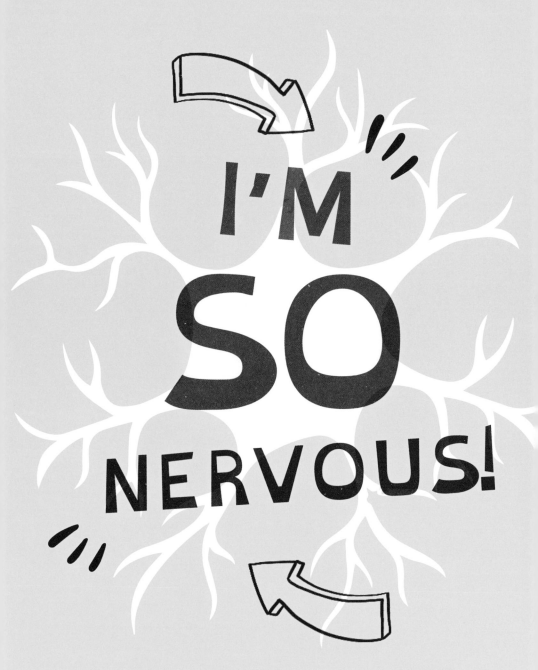

2

If your brain is like a supercomputer, then your nervous system is the network of wires connecting the supercomputer to everything it's in charge of. And just like real wires, this network runs on electricity too!

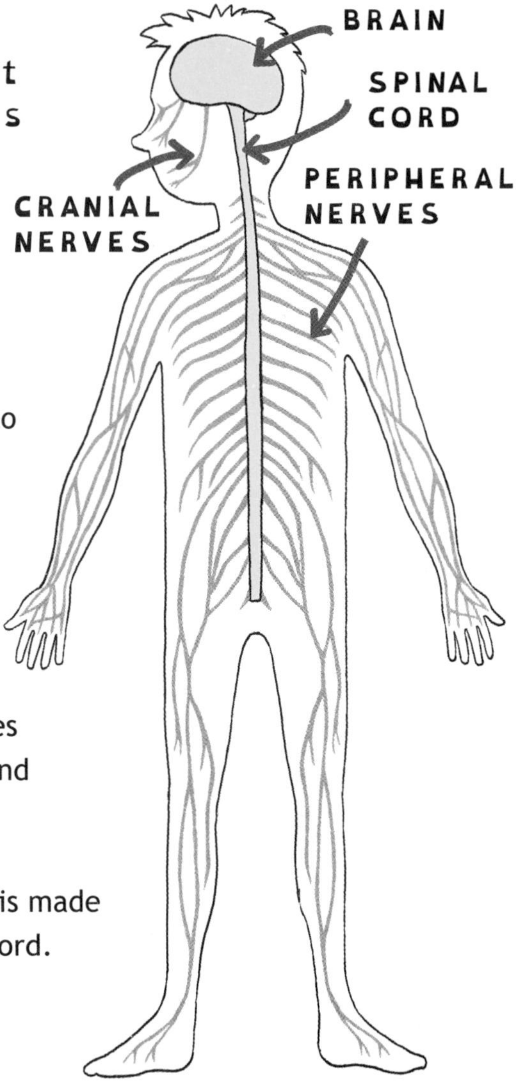

BRAIN

SPINAL CORD

PERIPHERAL NERVES

CRANIAL NERVES

Despite what it's called, the nervous system has nothing to do with you being worried about what your teacher will say when they find out your dog didn't really eat your homework. The nervous system is what we collectively call all the nerves that run around your body, and your brain is a part of it.

Your central nervous system is made up of your brain and spinal cord.

The brain is the main control centre of your nervous system and the spinal cord is the big bundle of wires coming out of it. Meanwhile, the peripheral nervous system is what we call the nerves between your spinal cord and different parts of your body. Think of them as the smaller wires coming off the main trunk. Each nerve is made of a bundle of smaller nerve cells (or neurons).

INSIDE A NERVE

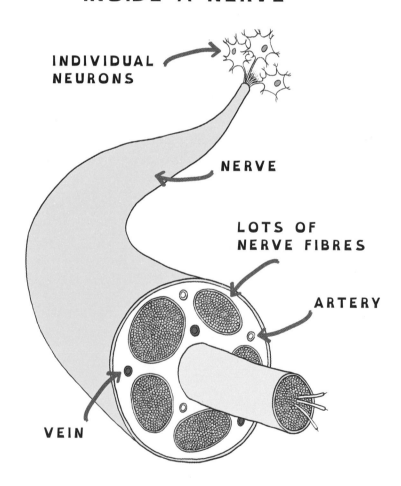

INDIVIDUAL NEURONS

NERVE

LOTS OF NERVE FIBRES

ARTERY

VEIN

YOUR OWN INFORMATION SUPERHIGHWAY

Your nervous system is a superhighway for information travelling to and from your brain. So when you want to kick a football, your brain sends a message down your spinal cord. This then travels out down a peripheral nerve to your leg. It tells your leg to kick, and off you go. **GOAL!**

However, if you miss the ball and your foot hits the ground and you stub your toe instead, your foot sends a pain message back through a peripheral nerve and up the spinal cord again. When it gets to your brain, that's when you sense that your toe hurts ... **OUCH**.

It sounds like it would take ages, and if you were sending the messages by post it probably would. But the electrical messages in your nervous system travel at lightning-fast speeds so they get to their destination unbelievably quickly.

How do we know this? It was two scientists called Alan Hodgkin and Andrew Huxley who worked out how neurons carry electricity. From 1939 to 1952 they did experiments on squids. I know, that seems like a really random choice of animal, but there was a reason: squids have really chunky neurons compared

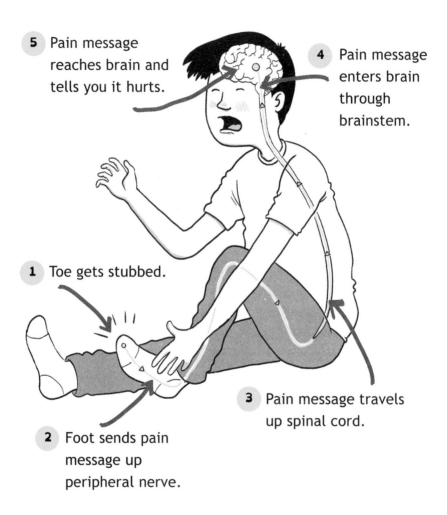

5 Pain message reaches brain and tells you it hurts.

4 Pain message enters brain through brainstem.

1 Toe gets stubbed.

3 Pain message travels up spinal cord.

2 Foot sends pain message up peripheral nerve.

to humans. That meant that they could attach equipment to them without it just slipping off. They were then able to show how the electrical signals travelled along the nerves. It turns out that it's all down to the movement of substances called sodium and potassium. So nothing like how the electricity travels around the wires in your home! For some reason the scientists in their laboratory liked to throw the giant squid nerves up at the ceiling after they were finished with them — and some of them are still there stuck to the ceiling seventy years later!

Your neurons come in all shapes and sizes. Some of them can be pretty big too. In fact, a single neuron running from the bottom of a grown-up's back to their big toe could be over a metre long! And humans aren't the only ones with long neurons. Did you know that a

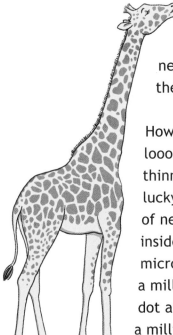

neuron running down a giraffe's neck to their toe can be several metres long?!

However, even though your neurons can be looooooooong, they're also extremely thin — thinner than a human hair, in fact. Which is lucky, because your body contains billions of neurons. They have to be small to fit inside you! They vary in size from 5 to 100 microns wide. How big is a micron? Well, it's a millimetre divided a thousand times. The dot at the top of this letter 'i' is around half a millimetre wide. That's 500 microns. So you could fit anywhere between 5 to 100 neurons side by side on it!

LET'S GET HANDS-ON

Your brain and the rest of your nervous system covering the different parts of your body all work together to make sense of the world around you. For example, when you stroke your pet cat, your brain knows how it feels because your hand is touching it and because your eyes can see it. Both your hands and eyes are sending information to your brain. It then puts it all together to tell you that your cat feels soft and furry. And at the same time, your cat's brain is telling it you are stroking it and it likes it too!

So your brain and nervous system are pretty smart, but there are ways to trick them. One of the coolest ways is called the 'phantom hand experiment'. Don't worry, a ghost isn't about to grab you! This experiment is all about fooling the brain into thinking that an object is actually part of your body when it isn't.

For this you will need to find a plastic fake hand and a friend to help.

Here's how to do it:

1) Ask a friend to sit opposite you at a small table.

2) Put both of your hands in front of you — your right one on top of the table and your left one below the table where you can't see it.

3) Put the fake hand in front of you where your left hand would be if it was on the table.

4) Ask your friend to repeatedly stroke or tap the fake hand (which you can see).

5) At the same time, ask them to repeatedly tap and stroke the hand that you cannot see under the table, in exactly the same way.

6) After about thirty seconds, something strange will happen: you will start to think that the fake hand actually belongs to you. It will feel like the tapping and stroking feeling is coming from the fake hand! This is because your brain is tying the two bits of information together: the signal from your hand under the table and your eyes seeing the fake hand on top of the table.

CONGRATULATIONS! You've successfully managed to fool your brain! Luckily your brain soon realises that the fake hand isn't yours when you stop the experiment. So don't worry, no one is about to walk off with your hand!

If you don't have a fake hand to hand (ha!), you can use a different object instead, but it's harder to fool your brain into playing along. Try it — see if you can trick your brain into thinking that your hand is actually an apple!

DANGER, DANGER!

Your brain and nervous system work closely together and are basically different parts of the same thing. However, sometimes your peripheral nervous system needs to ignore your brain completely!

Even though your brain is the control centre of the nervous system, it can be bypassed. You have automatic responses built in — especially when your safety is at risk. For instance, if you accidentally touch something really hot (like your mum's steaming cup of coffee), you immediately snatch your hand back before you even realise it's hot. This is called a reflex arc.

It happens because the nerves in your hand send a signal shooting towards your brain to tell you that you've touched something that's really hot and could hurt you. However, to save time, the signal hits the spinal cord which then immediately sends a message back down a different nerve to tell your hand to pull away as quickly as possible. This is before the message has even made it up to your brain!

WATCH OUT FOR TRAFFIC JAMS

Ever had that strange feeling of pins and needles in your hands or feet when you've been sitting in a funny position? First your foot goes numb and then it feels really tingly or prickly. Well, there's a really good reason why this happens, and it's down to your information superhighway.

When you sit on your hand or foot, it squashes the nerves that carry information back to your brain. This causes a bit of a traffic jam in the signals that are trying to go from your hand or foot back to your brain to tell you what you are feeling. Because the signals get stuck, you don't feel anything and your hand or foot goes numb.

Then, as the nerve slowly recovers, it starts to create signals randomly. These are felt as uncomfortable pins and needles. Fortunately, it soon goes away and you can feel everything again. **PHEW!**

THE TIME MY BRAIN
WENT A BIT WRONG...

I've had my own share of nerve trouble too. One of the nerves (called the facial nerve) which carries messages to and from one side of my face started to play up. It turns out an artery (these carry blood around the body from the heart) nearby was rubbing against the nerve, which made it fire off electrical signals for no reason. Unfortunately, I felt this as a really bad pain in my face (it even made me stop talking which is no mean feat!). I tried taking medicine for it to calm the nerve down, but when that stopped working, I had to have an operation.

The brain surgeon (called a neurosurgeon) was a lovely gentleman called Mr Sinan Barazi. He operated on my brain while I was under anaesthetic (medicine which kept me asleep so I didn't feel anything). He opened up a little hole in my skull and put a piece of special material called Teflon between the nerve and the artery so they couldn't touch each other.

It feels kind of cool that I have a material inside my head which has also been used in nuclear reactors.

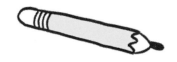

TOUCHY FEELY ...

Did you know that different parts of your body have different numbers of nerves in them? The more nerve endings that a particular part has, the more sensitive it is. For example, your fingertips have lots of nerve endings which is why you are able to sense so much by touching. That's why some blind or visually impaired people use Braille, an alphabet that you read by touching. However, the skin on your back, for example, doesn't have quite so many nerves and is less sensitive.

A really cool way to test this is with the two-point discrimination test (ooooh, sounds fancy!). We actually use this test in hospital to see if someone is having problems with their nervous system.

All you need is two pencils (make sure they are not too sharp!). Put the pencils side by side about 1 cm apart, close your eyes and touch both tips with your finger at the same time. You should be able to feel two separate points. If you put the tips closer together, they will start to feel like one.

Ask a friend to carefully do the same thing on the middle of your back. They should start with the pencils

side by side and gently press the tips against your skin.
It should feel as if they are one pencil at first. However,
if your friend gradually increases the space between
the pencils, you'll start to feel the two separate points.
This usually doesn't happen until they're at least a few
centimetres apart — much more than in your fingers!

The reason why this works is because there are more nerve endings closer together in your fingertips than there are in your back. Cool!

So now you're an expert in the nervous system. Everything we know is because of work done by some incredible people — like neuroscientists (people who study the brain and nerves), neurologists (doctors who look after those who have problems with their brain or nervous system), physiologists (scientists who work out how everything in the body works) and even zoologists (people who are experts in animals). Perhaps this chapter has inspired you to become one of those incredible people too! Just remember to mention me when you become world-famous for your amazing discoveries ...

3

By now, you might be thinking: hang on, Ranj, if we all have the same kinds of brains, made from the same kinds of neurons, connected to the same kinds of nervous systems, then how come we are all different?

Well, that's because our brains may look similar, but every single one of us has our own personality and our own mind. And everyone is just as important and incredible as anyone else — that includes you! You are unique; one of a kind.

Even if you haven't heard anyone say it today, you are special. And I'm going to tell you why ...

I THINK, THEREFORE I AM

Remember that clever guy René Descartes I mentioned earlier? He was the French philosopher who lived in the

1600s. That's long before your phone, television or even trains were invented! Philosophers are people who spend a lot of time thinking. Descartes spent all day thinking about our place in the universe and writing about it. If you looked him up, you'd find his famous quote: **I THINK, THEREFORE I AM.** What does that mean? Well, he was trying to say that the only reason he knew that he was real was because he was thinking about it. In other words: I am thinking, so I must be real. Oooof. I knew there was a reason why I'm a doctor and not a philosopher!

I THINK, THEREFORE I AM.

One of the other big ideas that René Descartes came up with was that the brain and the mind are actually different things. Your brain sits inside your skull and is constantly firing off and receiving electrical signals that control and sense what your body does. But your mind is the word we use to describe who you are, what you're thinking and how you're feeling.

Think of it like this: just because you have a brain, that doesn't automatically mean that you have a mind. Animals have brains like us, but they don't necessarily think, feel and behave like we do.

It is our minds that separate us from animals — and that is part of what being human is all about!

We've learned a bit more since Descartes was around, thanks to science. We now know that the mind definitely comes from the brain. So your brain isn't just the control centre of the body. It also decides who you are as well as the kinds of things you like doing (like painting, dancing or playing football). It even decides whether you are left- or right-handed!

LEFTIES AND RIGHTIES

Most people in the world are right-handed, meaning they write with their right hand and prefer to use their right hand for lots of other tasks. You might be one of the really special few who are left-handed — around one in ten of us are, and boys are more likely to be than girls. You might even be ambidextrous (meaning you use both hands in a similar way, rather than having a preference for one). But have you ever thought about *why* you are left- or right-handed? It turns out scientists have been wondering the same for ages too.

If you look at the brain as a whole, you'll see it's divided down the middle into two halves, called hemispheres. Each hemisphere is like a mirror image of the other, so you have two of everything in your brain, one on either side. And funnily, the left side of your brain controls the right side of your body, and vice versa!

Isn't that cool? So when you turn the next page, if you do it with your left hand, it's actually the right side of your brain telling your left hand what to do.

People who are right-handed use the left side of their brain more. People who are left-handed tend

BRAIN HEMISPHERES: TWO HALVES MAKE A WHOLE!

R   L   R   L

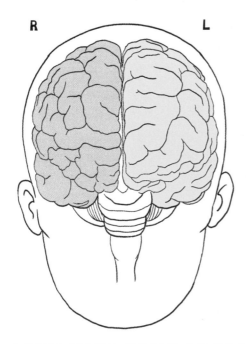

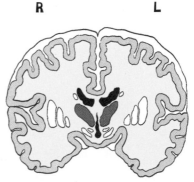

WHAT YOUR BRAIN LOOKS LIKE IN THE MIDDLE (LIKE A SLICE OF BREAD FROM THE MIDDLE OF A LOAF)

WHAT YOUR BRAIN LOOKS LIKE FROM THE FRONT

L   R

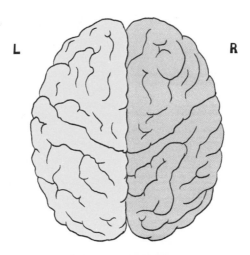

WHAT YOUR BRAIN LOOKS LIKE FROM ABOVE

to use both sides. This is because the two sides of the brain are slightly better connected in left-handers — especially in the areas that look after language. If you're lucky enough to be left-handed, you might even be more creative because of the way your brain works. So tell that to the next person who says you're using the wrong hand. You may just be a creative genius!

Your brain also likes to use different hemispheres for different things. Why? Because using both to do exactly the same thing would be a waste of time (and brains)! Think of it like bouncing a ball. Why use both hands to bounce it when you could just use one? That way, you can use your other hand to do something else ... like flipping a pancake!

BRAINS OR BRAWN?

Have you noticed that people are better at some things than others? Could it be true that some people are good at thinking tasks and others are better at doing things?

For instance, you may be amazing at picking up dance moves, but just can't get your head around learning algebra. When I was growing up, I found that things like art and music were quite easy for me, but I struggled with maths problems. My brother was awesome at drawing, but just wasn't keen on other subjects. Some people are amazing at sports and find subjects like science difficult.

Part of the reason for this is down to how your brain is wired — just like how left-handed people might naturally be more creative. But brains can change depending on how you use them, and on the things you do or that happen to you when you are growing up. Like how people used to think that boys' and girls' brains were nothing alike, but a lot of the differences we notice in how they behave is probably just because of what boys and girls are encouraged to do.

This is all due to something we call **NEUROPLASTICITY**. Even though your brain may be wired and put together a certain way to begin with, it is able to rewire and reorganise itself if needed. This is especially true when you are a child. But adults pick up new skills all the time too. Do you know any grown-ups who took up a new hobby during the COVID-19 lockdowns?

And here's the best bit: this means that you can train your brain, just like you can train your body. We all have some natural ability to do anything (some more than

others), but the rest of us can get better with practice. I got better at maths problems by learning the basics and then doing them over and over. Tamara Rojo is a world-famous ballet dancer and she trains for hours and hours every day to be the best. Judit Polgár is a Hungarian chess grandmaster, probably the best female chess master of all time, but she only got there through practice!

BRAINS AND INTELLIGENCE

OK, so you can train your brain to help you do things, but can you make it more clever? After all, everyone wants to be clever, right? We all want to know lots, do well at school and get good jobs when we're grown-ups.

You may have heard people using the word intelligence when they are talking about being clever. Around one hundred years ago, a French psychologist called Alfred Binet created a test to measure intelligence. He was asked to identify children who needed extra help at school. So he came up with a series of questions and problems to solve that gave an idea of how clever a child was.

The test has changed since then and these days it is called the IQ (or Intelligence Quotient) test. It gives people an IQ score to tell them how intelligent they might be compared to other people their own age. Marilyn vos Savant is an American author and she has one of the highest IQ scores ever recorded. At one point she was in the *Guinness Book of Records*! The IQ test can be completed by people of all ages, but the questions are different depending on the age of the person. In theory, your score should be the same if you take it when you're eight and when you're fifty-eight — because it's supposed to measure something constant about your level of cleverness.

But here's the thing: IQ tests are not perfect. Like playing chess or ballet dancing, it is possible to train yourself to get better at taking IQ tests by practising. But just because your score is increasing, that doesn't necessarily mean you are getting any more intelligent!

For a while, IQ tests were popular, but we don't really use them nowadays because they only demonstrate one particular way of being clever. There are actually many different types of intelligence. I know, mind blown, right? Being intelligent doesn't just mean being really good at mental arithmetic or being able to learn facts. Being intelligent means being able to use your brain to be good at something — and that something might be rocking out on guitar or knowing how to make someone feel better when they're sad.

In 1983, a psychologist called Howard Gardner came up with the idea that there are nine different types of intelligence. They have fancy names, but what they mean is quite straightforward:

MUSICAL

This means you're good at recognising and playing music. People like Beyoncé and Ed Sheeran fall into this group.

LOGICAL–MATHEMATICAL

You might be in this group if you love numbers, patterns and solving problems (like Albert Einstein or the famous Indian mathematician Shakuntala Devi).

BODILY KINAESTHETIC

If you fall into this group, you'll find sports and movement are your thing. Professional dancers definitely have a lot of this. Shirley Ballas, head judge on the TV show *Strictly Come Dancing*, is a world-class Latin and ballroom dancer and is a great example of this. Another one is DuShaunt 'Fik-shun' Stegall, who won the dance competition *So You Think You Can Dance* in 2013 at the age of eighteen. He is one of the best hip-hop dancers in the USA.

LINGUISTIC

This means you are good with words, languages and talking to others. People with linguistic intelligence are also great at writing and telling stories. Oprah Winfrey, one of my all-time favourite chat show hosts, has great linguistic intelligence. Also, look up a lady called Dr Maya Angelou, who was a famous writer and poet (as well as other things) who had the most amazing way with words.

INTERPERSONAL

Are you good at getting on with other people?
That probably means you have high interpersonal
intelligence. These people tend to do jobs that involve
dealing with other people a lot — like your teachers!

NATURALIST

Do you like being in nature? Do you like learning
facts about animals and plants? Then you might have
naturalist intelligence. I reckon lots of science teachers
have this.

SPATIAL

People with spatial intelligence like to visualise
things. They're particularly good at jigaw puzzles
and mazes. They're also pretty nifty with maps,
designing things and thinking about the way things
look. Famous photographers like Ian Rankin have lots
of spatial intelligence.

INTRAPERSONAL

This sounds really similar to interpersonal, but is a
different thing. People with intrapersonal intelligence
are really good at understanding their own emotions
and feelings, but also those of others. People with

intrapersonal intelligence are creative and have lots of empathy. Michelle Obama has loads of intrapersonal intelligence!

EXISTENTIAL

OK, this is one of the more tricky ones to describe. People with lots of existential intelligence like to think about the meaning of life and why we are all here. They like to learn about how humans have come about and where we might be going. They tend to be deep thinkers, poets, writers and philosophers — like René Descartes!

All this is helpful for showing us that there are lots of ways to be good at things, and that there isn't just one way to be intelligent. So if you struggle in school or feel like you don't do some things as well as your friends or family, that doesn't mean you aren't intelligent. It might mean that your strengths lie elsewhere. And one person can have many different types of intelligence, which means you can be good at a number of different things.

So, what types of intelligence do you have? What makes you a clever clogs? Grab a bit of paper and try out the quiz on the next page to see if it gives you a clue.

1

Do you like spending time in and learning about nature? Do you know lots about plants and animals?

YES

You might have **naturalist** intelligence. Write it down and move on to the next question.

NO

2

Do you like being around and talking to lots of different people? Do you find it easy to get on with others?

YES

You might have **interpersonal** intelligence. Write it down and move on to the next question.

NO

3

Do you love music? Do you find it easy to pick out the notes of a tune and play it back?

YES

You might have **musical** intelligence. Write it down and move on to the next question.

NO

4

Do you love working with numbers? Are you really good at solving puzzles?

YES

You might have **logical-mathematical** intelligence. Write it down and move on to the next question.

NO

5

Are you good at doing things with your hands? Can you learn a dance routine easily?

YES

You might have **bodily-kinaesthetic** intelligence. Write it down and move on to the next question.

NO ⟶ **GO TO QUESTION 6**

6

Do you like working with maps and instructions? Are you interested in mazes and jigsaw puzzles?

 YES

You might have **spatial** intelligence. Write it down and move on to the next question.

 NO

7

Are you good with words or at languages? Are you good at writing or telling stories?

 YES

You might have **linguistic** intelligence. Write it down and move on to the next question.

 NO

8

Do you like spending time by yourself and thinking things through? Are you good at understanding feelings and emotions?

 YES

You might have **intrapersonal** intelligence. Write it down and move on to the next question.

 NO

9

Do you like thinking about the meaning of life and why we are here?

 YES

You might have **existential** intelligence. Write it down.

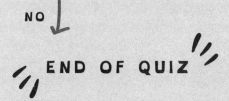 NO

END OF QUIZ

Look at your piece of paper now and you should have an idea about what types of intelligence you have!

Once you know what your strengths are, you can use them for your benefit. It can also help you feel more confident about doing things related to them. However, that doesn't mean you shouldn't feel confident about doing anything else. We don't definitively know what gives a person a particular type of intelligence. It's likely to be partly due to what they are born with and how their brain is put together (nature) and partly what happens to them when they grow up and how the brain organises itself over time (nurture). Remember neuroplasticity? You can train yourself to get better at the things you find more challenging. Practice makes perfect. That's how I finally learned my times tables! In the next chapter I've got loads of great tips and tricks for you to help train your brain in the things you aren't so good at.

WE ALL WORK IN DIFFERENT WAYS

As we now know, brains may all look similar but every one works slightly differently. Each one (and each person) is unique. That means there is something called a spectrum — a wide range in how different brains can be.

Some people's brains work very differently to others'.

This is called neurodiversity — a fancy word that just means 'different brains'. Neurodiverse people have brains that work quite differently to many other people's. We don't know why this happens for certain, but neurodiverse people have always been around. Neurodiversity is something you are born with. It's probably down to the way the brain is put together, rather than something you have developed over time.

There are lots of different kinds of neurodiversity. I've explained a few of them below, but there are many others too — you might want to go away and learn about them yourself. Over the next few pages I've asked some neurodiverse people to share their experiences of growing up — because it's always better to listen to people with direct knowledge of something if you can.

ADHD

One of the important things about learning is that it helps if you focus and concentrate. This can be tricky if the topic is a really boring one. It can also be tough for people who have something called ADHD, or attention deficit hyperactivity disorder. If you have ADHD, you might find it really hard to keep your thoughts and actions under control. Your mind might always go wandering whenever you're trying to concentrate on something, so it takes you a long time to complete tasks. You might find it difficult to stop yourself doing things that could get you into trouble. You might also have lots of energy all the time and find it hard to get to sleep.

My family didn't know it at the time, but looking back I think my brother probably had ADHD growing up. Why? Well, he found it hard to sit still and concentrate on one thing, he'd do or say things without thinking about them first, and he was always on the go! It was like his brain was running at 100 kilometres per hour!

Luckily there are things that can help people with ADHD. This could include changing the way you do things to make them more manageable. There's also talking therapy, where you speak to a specialist who helps you control your thoughts and actions better. For others it could mean taking medication which helps you to feel calmer.

Children with ADHD often get told that they are naughty, which can make them feel like their ADHD is always a problem or that they aren't good at anything. This isn't true. Find something you're good at and practise focusing on that, and then you can show others your strengths. For my brother, his strength was drawing. He is an awesome artist!

CREATIVE CONNECTIONS
by Tara Chakraborty

As a school kid, I was a bit shy, quiet and daydreamy. If you were in my classroom, you would often find me gazing out of windows and doodling during lessons. Back then, I did not feel very confident and if someone had told me that I was good at something, I probably wouldn't have believed them. My teachers used to tell me off all the time for not paying attention and even though I tried really hard, I usually found it very difficult to stay on task and focus on schoolwork both at school and at home.

However, art, music and anything creative came very easily to me and I would often spend hours drawing, painting, writing and making all kinds of things and I got increasingly good at doing that. Looking back, I can see that having those creative outlets really helped me through that time, even though I often used them to avoid doing something else!

I was diagnosed with ADHD two years ago, when I was fifteen years old. Even though I felt a bit sad at first about being labelled as 'different', I was mostly just very relieved to finally understand why I struggled with so many things that other people did not. Since then, I have learned a lot about my ADHD, and I have even done a research project at school about it. Knowing what things work for me (and what things really don't) is really useful and I find schoolwork easier now. I have also come to really appreciate the great strengths that having ADHD can bring. I really love all things creative and spending time on them is never a chore. My brain likes the freedom of bending the rules and making unusual connections. As I naturally jump from one thing to another, I am never short of a new idea when I need one.

My ADHD has also caused me to prioritise exploring and developing my creativity and the things that I am most passionate about. I have won prizes for my art; I really enjoy performing my own music and I know that being involved in the arts will be part of my future. I think that it is no accident that so many successful creative people that I look up to have ADHD. Their achievements, innovating and entertaining inspire me to see ADHD not as a problem but as a real and unique strength.

DYSLEXIA

People who have dyslexia have trouble with reading and writing because their brain sees words in different ways. Because of this, it can take them longer to read something or they may not spell easily, which can make school feel more difficult sometimes. But that doesn't stop dyslexic people from being amazing. You might struggle with words, but perhaps you are brilliantly musical. You might also be really good at solving problems because you think in different ways to other people. Again, find your strengths — there's always something!

Famous people with dyslexia include the awesome space scientist Dr Maggie Aderin-Pocock, who is probably one of the coolest people I have ever met!

DYSCALCULIA AND DYSPRAXIA

People who have dyscalculia struggle with numbers and may find maths and arithmetic difficult. Those with dyspraxia find moving in a co-ordinated way tricky (co-ordination is the way your muscles work together). So they may bump into things or fall over more. However, you might also be better at other things — some people with dyscalculia will be really good at creative stuff, and those with dyspraxia may be great at remembering things.

AUTISM

Autistic people (like my beautiful little nephew Rohan) have brains that think quite differently. They might find it harder to fit in with others, so may prefer to spend time by themselves or only with certain people. They don't always find it easy to understand what others are thinking or feeling. Autistic people might see things quite literally, which can make stuff like jokes difficult to understand. They may also like very specific things or want to do things in a certain way, and if that doesn't happen, they might feel really uncomfortable. Sometimes they can feel overwhelmed and may need to take themselves away for a while or take a time-out.

At the same time, autistic people can be incredible at certain skills and subjects. They may be brilliant at learning to speak lots of different languages. They may be talented artists. They may also be able to remember things really easily or know lots about certain things. Satoshi Tajiri, the guy who created Pokémon, is autistic — he got the idea for the game from his love of collecting bugs. He actually wanted to grow up and become an entomologist (an expert in bugs) but he's now the inventor of one of the best video games in the world!

THE RULES OF COOL

by Catrin Lawrence

Back when I was in primary school (and people went to the shops on dinosaurs), I was very concerned about being 'cool' and fitting in. I already knew back then that, as an autistic person, other people might not see me as 'cool'. I already knew some kids saw me as downright weird.

One day, I asked my best friend how to reach this elusive goal of coolness. I can't remember everything she told me, but here are some highlights:

- *Don't walk with your arms folded*
- *Say 'puke' instead of 'vomit'*
- *Never carry your jumper over your arm — it must always be round your waist (even if it gets you in trouble with the teachers)*

Even back then, I found these rules . . . odd. Why did it matter if I said vomit instead of puke? How did my arms show how cool I was? Why couldn't I be cool and not get in trouble with my teachers? In the end, I don't think I took much of my friend's advice.

Now I'm twenty-three and wrinkly, I've realised something about these rules. They didn't mean

anything to me, but to my non-autistic friend, they were the difference between being seen as cool . . . or strange. Usually, it's us autistic people who are seen as anxious to fit in or to not be seen as 'different'. However, non-autistic, or neurotypical, people are just as worried about fitting in, perhaps even more so than us! Next time you're worried about not being cool, or not knowing how to be cool, just know that nobody really knows.

And nobody cares if you say 'vomit'.

Just like everyone else, not all autistic people are the same. For some, being autistic makes no difference to their life at all. Others may needs lots of help and support with everyday things. There is a huge variety and that's why people sometimes call it the 'autistic spectrum'.

If you are neurodiverse, I want you to know that there's nothing wrong — it's just another thing that makes you unique. I know people might treat you differently because of it and that can be hard — it can make you feel different, or less confident. That's their issue, not yours. Like anyone else, people who are neurodiverse have things that they are good at and things that they might need extra help with.

Everyone has challenges, whether they are neurodiverse or not — yours are just a bit different. Always remember that your neurodiversity is a part of you, and you can use it as a strength. It doesn't have to prevent you from achieving your dreams. In fact, some of the most famous and successful people in history are neurodiverse!

CEREBRAL PALSY

Let's move on to some other things that can change the way your brain works.

As a doctor, I sometimes look after children who were born with medical conditions that affect their brains. These conditions are different to neurodiversity because in these cases, the brain isn't able to work like it should.

Cerebral palsy is where part of the brain becomes damaged and can't do its job properly. Sometimes this happens just before or around the time the person is born. It can affect you in different ways — some people might have a slight problem with their movement, some may need a wheelchair to get about, and others may not be able to move or speak at all.

I once worked with a lady called Rosie Jones, who is one of the funniest people I have ever met. Rosie has cerebral palsy and it takes her a bit longer to move around and speak. Still, being playful with words is what she's especially awesome at — Rosie is one of the most popular comedians in the UK. But my favourite thing about her is that she found it funny when I covered her in gunge as part of a children's TV show!

OBSTACLES

by Kay Channon

I was always early for English. Due to being born with cerebral palsy, I needed to use a wheelchair. So in the classroom, I had to park perfectly so that it didn't become an inconvenient obstacle if anyone needed the toilet during the lesson. My desk was higher than the others and instead of a nice smooth wooden finish, it

had lots of dents on its surface. I remember arriving one morning to find someone had carved 'What am I doing here?' in the top corner and being surprised that I could read it despite the letters being upside down because at the time, I didn't realise I was dyslexic.

My teaching assistant would then slide discreetly into a seat nearby before the glamour-obsessed texting clan arrived. The glamour clan never liked me. We never said more than ten words to each other throughout the entire school year, they just thought that sitting to the side of the classroom (as I did) would make their texting activities less obvious. They would often whisper about me 'cheating' or being 'lucky because I had a helper'. Nothing could be further from the truth.

A firm push of the door and a flash of flimsy cardboard folders meant the arrival of my teacher and a new obstacle — note taking. Central themes in Jane Eyre. *I could only remember five words written on the board before having to remind myself what the next part of the sentence said. My dyslexia was messing with my writing again . . . 'What was between love and loneliness?' Who knows?! My teacher had already made use of the eraser and moved on. I actually liked English, but there was just so much to remember and the stiffness in my hands made writing very slow. My spelling wasn't much better, so my teaching assistant would take notes in the lesson too. It wasn't always easy to read their handwriting, but I found a way to make understanding their notes easier — highlighters! I chose yellow for poetry, green for plays (usually Shakespeare) and pink for novels.*

This system received a lot of criticism from the glamour clan, but it really helped, especially when organising my homework. Whilst I may not have gained the marks I wished for in my final exam, I was very proud to be given the award for English at the end of the school year.

EPILEPSY

Another medical brain condition is epilepsy. This is where the neurons of the brain become really excitable and start to fire off electrical signals when they shouldn't. The results of this can be pretty random and even frightening. Epileptic people have fits or seizures where they might start to act strangely all of a sudden, may go completely blank and just stare, a part of their body might start shaking uncontrollably, or they might fall to the ground and their whole body starts shaking.

If your friend has epilepsy and has a fit, then it's important to get help and tell a grown-up. If you have epilepsy, then make sure you take your medicines properly and let those around you know what to do in case you have a fit.

No matter your type of intelligence, whether you are neurodiverse, or whether you have a particular brain condition, always remember that we all have things that we find difficult. And we all have things that we are good at. We are all awesome in our own way. Find your strengths and make the most of them!

4

Time to get down to business! Now you've got to know your own awesome brain, how do you make it even better? Because just like you can train your pet dog to do cool tricks, you can train your brain to do incredible things as well. It just takes time and practice!

I'm not talking about teaching yourself how to fetch or jump over fences (but you can do that too if you like). I mean things like training yourself to learn better, to be

able to remember stuff so you can ace tests at school, to have faster reactions so you can be the best athlete in the world, and to look after your mind to keep it happy and healthy.

CAN YOU MAKE YOUR BRAIN STRONGER?

YES, YOU CAN! First, by making sure you exercise your brain every day. Exercising your body makes it stronger, fitter and healthier — and the same goes for your mind!

Don't worry, that doesn't involve taking your brain out of your head and running it on a treadmill. Simply making sure you use your brain to do different things helps keep it active.

For example:

1) **DOING PUZZLES** — jigsaws, crosswords and even maths puzzles are all great because they exercise parts of the brain that look after complex thinking, pattern recognition and reasoning, making them stronger. So the next time you have to solve a problem on a test at school, your brain should be better prepared.

2) **READING BOOKS** — any kind of book is fine, from a book packed with facts to your favourite picture book or story. So you can tell your parents that a doctor has told you to read more comics!

3) **BEING CREATIVE** — why not take up some arts or crafts? I used to love learning how to do origami as a kid. That's the Japanese art of paper-folding. Good for your brain and you could make yourself some really cool paper figurines!

There are also some fun activities you can try especially to train your brain. This is really putting your neurons through their paces!

ON THE MOVE

Try this when you're on your way to school. If you notice someone walking by on the street, pick out three things about them. For example, what clothes they're wearing, their hair colour and what kind of bag they have. Then after they've gone, wait five minutes and see how many of those three things you can remember. The more you practise this, the better you'll get. Remember not to shout your three things out loud though ... you'll get some funny looks!

MEMORY STORY

Ask a friend to come up with a list of random words for you. After reading the list for 30 seconds, can you remember all the words? If so, ask your friend to make a new list including a couple more words! When it starts getting tricky, try linking the words together in a story. For example, if the words are: mouse, apple, car, shoe, balloon, puddles, you might find it hard to remember them all quickly just as they are. But try making a story, like: 'the mouse was eating an apple while sitting in his car on the way to work, but realised he'd forgotten his shoe and so he used a balloon to float away so that his feet didn't get wet in the puddles'. I know it sounds ridiculous, but it works! How long a list of words can you remember?

FAST MATHS

Want to be better at doing multiplication quickly in your head? Try my fast maths exercise.

Get yourself a piece of paper and draw out a table like the one below — 13 columns by 13 rows. Write the numbers 1—12 in the first column and first row. Then in the remaining boxes, write down the multiplication of the numbers at the top of the columns and the start of the rows. For example, the number 6 goes in the third row/fourth column box because it is 2 x 3. Like this:

	1	2	3	4	5	6	7	8	9	10	11	12
1	1	2	3	4								
2	2	4	6	8								
3	3	6	9									
4	4											
5												
6												
7												
8												
9												
10												
11												
12												

The idea is to time how long it takes for you to complete the whole table. Then see if you can go faster next time!

If that's too easy, try jumbling up the numbers in the first row and column so they're not in order — this is really difficult. You could even have a race against your friends!

INVISIBLE ALPHABET

This is another game to play with your friends. It tests your hand-eye co-ordination as well as your ability to multitask, or do several things at once.

Put both your arms out in front of you and draw a letter from the alphabet with your right hand. Then draw a different letter with your left hand. Easy, right? Now draw the two different letters at the same time with both hands! For example, draw an 'f' with your left hand while drawing a 't' with your right.

You and a friend could set each other challenges with different letters to see who gets the most right. If you want to be really clever, try short words!

WORD SCRAMBLE

This is a great way to learn new words and also brush up on your spelling. Ask a friend to choose a word and write it down on some paper (you can use a dictionary if you like). Make sure they space the letters out when writing them down. You're allowed to take one look at the word before the next step. Next ask your friend to cut each letter out and scramble them up. Then see if you can reassemble the word by yourself. You can pick longer and more difficult words as you get better!

LEARN FOR LIFE . . .

I've spent A LOT of my life learning. At school, then university, then being a doctor, and even learning scripts for TV shows. Did I tell you that I sometimes appear on TV? Anyway, I like to think I've got pretty good at it now. But I've definitely learned some useful tricks along the way!

Learning is important because it makes us better at the things we have to do, and also the things we like to do. I know going to school can sometimes be a pain, or seem boring, but this is crucial learning you are doing that could lay the groundwork for the job of your dreams. All the reading and writing you have been doing might help you become an author (just like me writing this book!).

The maths problems you're working on right now could help you invent a new form of energy to power cars. Learning science could mean that you become an astronaut and travel to a distant planet on a space expedition. Doing music and drama lessons may land you with an Oscar or a Grammy one day!

You're taking in so much new stuff every day at school. And the truth is, you never really stop learning. Even though I work as a doctor, I still learn new things every day so that I can stay up to date and know the latest treatments for my patients.

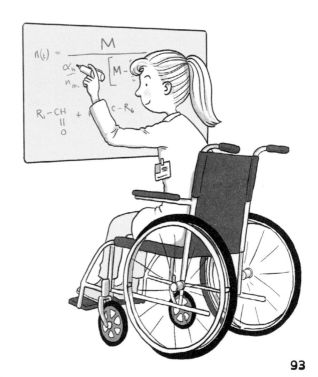

DIFFERENT KINDS OF LEARNERS

To learn, you have to be able to take new information in and store it in your brain. That way, you can use it at a later time. But did you know that there are different kinds of learners? Similar to how we talked about different kinds of intelligence in the last chapter, there are different ways to learn too.

There are four kinds of learner — see if you can work out which one you are using this quiz:

Which of these do you find easiest to remember?

a)   Something you've seen, like a picture or diagram.

b)   Something you've heard, like the words to a song.

c)   Something you've read, like a book or handout.

d)   Something you've done, like a science experiment.

Which method would you pick if you had to learn some information?

a) Drawing a picture or chart.

b) Listening to a recording of it.

c) Writing it down.

d) Walking around while you learn.

What kind of work do you enjoy most in school?

a) Art projects.

b) Music.

c) Reading and writing.

d) Science experiments.

Do you find it easier to learn when your teacher:

a) Draws a diagram on the board or shows a picture?

b) Reads something out loud to the class?

c) Gives you a handout to read?

d) Gets you to do an activity or exercise that involves moving around?

MOSTLY As

You might be **VISUAL** learner. This is someone who learns better using pictures or diagrams.

MOSTLY Bs

You might be an **AUDITORY** learner. This is someone who learns by hearing things out loud.

MOSTLY Cs

You might be a **READING/WRITING** learner. This is someone who learns by reading and writing things down.

MOSTLY Ds

You might be a **KINAESTHETIC** learner. This is someone who learns better by moving around or touching things.

It's quite likely that you fall into more than one of these groups — over half of us will! I've discovered that if I'm learning medical stuff, I'm better with diagrams and pictures — so that makes me a visual learner. If I need to learn a piece of music or a song, then I am an auditory learner. And if I need to learn a script or film for TV, then I actually become a kinaesthetic learner. You'll often find me walking around talking to myself!

Try it for yourself. The next time you're learning something off by heart for school, like lines for a play, try one of the different learning styles mentioned above and see which works best for you. Or if you're studying for a science test, see if putting the information in a different way helps you remember facts more easily.

A mind map is a diagram you can create to learn words or information. It's a bit like a tree. Here's how to do it: start by writing the heading in the middle of the page, then create 'branches' from that, with a main piece of information on each one. Then create smaller branches off those with other information. Have a look at this example . . .

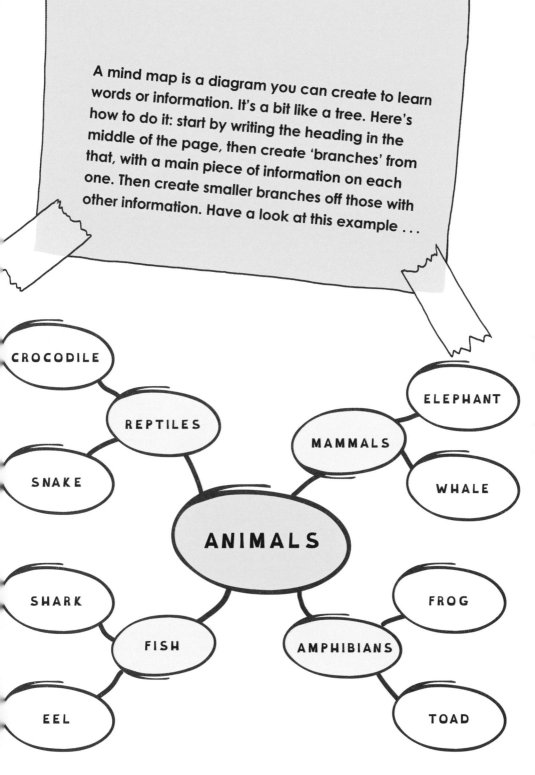

EXTRA LEARNING NEEDS

Not everyone finds it easy to learn. You may have heard some people using the words 'learning difficulties'. This phrase is often used to describe people who may have extra learning needs or need a bit more help at school.

Knowing that you need extra support can make you feel less confident or as if you aren't as good as others. But remember: even if you're getting extra help at school, that doesn't mean you're not super-talented. No one is good at everything! It's about finding and building the skills you enjoy or are good at!

For example, I remember meeting a little boy with Down syndrome, a condition he was born with which can make you look a certain way and can involve some medical problems. Some people with Down syndrome also have learning difficulties and they need extra help in class. This little boy went to a special school to get that support. But his superpower was dancing — I got to see him perform and he was incredible! Finding his passion had made him so happy, and it made everyone around him happy too because it was so clear he was having a brilliant time. So if you're ever struggling with something, don't forget: we all have things we find tough, and other things we're **AMAZING** at.

PRACTICE MAKES PERFECT

To learn, our brains have to be able to store information. We do this by making memories — just like a computer stores things in its memory. Thankfully, we don't stop working if we accidentally spill a glass of water over ourselves — but your computer might not be quite so lucky!

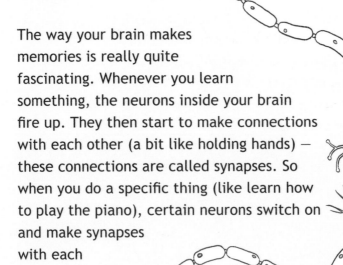

The way your brain makes memories is really quite fascinating. Whenever you learn something, the neurons inside your brain fire up. They then start to make connections with each other (a bit like holding hands) — these connections are called synapses. So when you do a specific thing (like learn how to play the piano), certain neurons switch on and make synapses with each other, and they stay linked together, helping the memory get stored.

If you want to get really good at something, then doing it over and over again is key. I took part in a TV show called *Strictly Come Dancing* for which I had to learn a brand-new dance every week and then perform it in front of the whole nation. Yep, it was pretty scary stuff! The day before the big performance, my partner Janette (who is an awesome dancer, by the way), used to make us run through the whole routine ten times in a row. Why? Because it helped me remember it.

When we do something over and over again, the connections in our brain get stronger and we can remember it more quickly and easily. In fact, after a while the connections can become so strong that you can do it without even thinking about it. Some people call this 'muscle memory', but it's nothing to do with storing memories in your muscles at all!

I never got a perfect score for my dances, but the repetition meant that I hardly ever forgot a dance step. Janette has been dancing for years and she gets it right every single time. So there you go. Practice really does make perfect!

MY TOP TESTING TIPS

Do you struggle to learn new things? Do you find it hard to focus or concentrate? Have you got a big audition or test that you're worried about?

I've learned lots of neat tricks from all my years of studying that are perfect for helping you ace tests, and these are my top five tips:

1) **CREATE A LEARNING SPACE**

   You know how your parents are always telling you to tidy up your room? Well, it's not just so that it looks nice and clean when your granny pops round. Making sure that the space you study in is organised and not too cluttered means there are fewer distractions and you can concentrate better. A tidy room means a tidy mind!

2) **FUEL YOUR BRAIN**

   This is all about giving your brain the things it needs to work properly. So try not to do your homework on an empty stomach (hunger always puts me off), make sure you drink enough water (remember, your brain is mostly water), and get enough sleep (we'll talk about this more in the next chapter).

3) PREPARE AND PLAN

If you've got a lot of things to learn, try to divide them up into smaller things and make a plan for what you're going to do and when. You could even create a learning timetable for yourself. Breaking bigger tasks into smaller ones gives your brain a chance to take in and sort the information better. There's less for your brain to cope with at one time. And having a structure or pattern to your learning makes it feel less daunting.

4) PRACTICE

Now that you have a better idea about what kind of learner you are (using the quiz on page 94), you can pick a method of taking in information that works for you, and then keep doing it! For example, try creating a chart or making colourful notes or diagrams when learning facts. Or try moving around when learning lists of things or dialogue for a play. Then the more you go over it, the more likely it is to stay in your head.

5) TEST YOURSELF

Why not test yourself to see how much you can remember? Or you and your friends could test each other. Talking things through helps you understand them better and remember them.

Now that you've tried my brain-training exercises, why not try to come up with some of your own? Then you could try them out on your friends and see how good they are at them. You could even create your own little manual full of tips and exercises you find helpful — and then go over it now and again to keep your brain fighting fit!

5

If I've done my job properly, you'll now understand why your brain is one of the most important organs inside your body. No matter who you are or how your brain works, it's essential to make the most of it so that you can be the very best you can be.

In the last chapter we learned some brain exercises you could use to supercharge that supercomputer inside your head. However, to get the most out of it, you need to care for your mind as well.

Being happy and comfortable in who you are, to help you make the most out of every day, is just as important as being good at hobbies and doing well at school. I believe that how you think and feel is just as important as what you know and do. It's also crucial to know what to do if things aren't going so well and you're finding life a bit hard. If you can get better at this mental health stuff right now, it will help you as

you grow up, become a teenager, become a grown-up
... and even when you get a bit old and wrinkly!

BOUNCE BACK

When something difficult has happened, it's really
important to be able to find a way to bounce back — to
get back to feeling like yourself again so it doesn't keep
you down for too long. This skill is called resilience.
Another way of thinking about resilience is as a type of
strength. If we can make our minds stronger, we'll be
able to cope better with everyday life.

Resilience is important for lots of reasons:

1)   It helps you to cope with difficult feelings better.

2)   It helps you get through stressful times in your life.

3)   It helps you to learn from your mistakes and be
     better in future.

4)   It helps you to support other people when they're
     in need of a helping hand.

So I hope you can see why I think resilience is key
to growing up happy. The reason why I'm telling you
all this is because all of the information and tips in
this chapter will help you to improve your mental

resilience — starting with one of the most important: sleep.

SWITCH OFF AND RECHARGE

You might sometimes feel like being asleep is just wasting time when you could be having fun. But in fact, sleep is one of the most important things that we do. That's why we spend around one-third of our lives asleep. Just think, if you're nine years old, that means you've been asleep for a total of three years already!

Sleep doesn't just help your tired muscles to rest after a day of running around on the playing field. It does the same for your brain too. But when you sleep, your brain doesn't completely switch off. In fact, three really cool things happen:

1) Your brain releases chemicals called hormones which help control various processes inside your body. For example, it makes something called melatonin, which helps you drift off to sleep. It also releases growth hormone, which helps your body grow and repair itself.

2) Your brain sorts out the information that it has absorbed during the day and decides what it needs to keep and what it can get rid of. The stuff it keeps gets stored as memories.

3) After a day of working hard, your brain gets rid of waste products from its cells that it doesn't need — a bit like putting trash down a rubbish chute.

If you get a good night's sleep, your brain will be in great shape to concentrate and learn at school the next day. You'll also be better at dealing with stress and worry — sleep helps your mental health and resilience.

HOW MUCH SLEEP DO YOU REALLY NEED?

You might have heard that people need eight hours of sleep a night, but the truth is that we're all different. Some people need lots of sleep and others seem to get by on very little. I'm definitely a person that likes snoozing!

As a general rule, the younger you are, the more sleep you need because you do more growing. Babies spend a lot of time asleep because their brains and bodies are growing so much. Grown-ups sleep much less. The average six to thirteen year old needs between nine and eleven hours' sleep every night.

An easy way to know if you're getting enough sleep each night is to see how you're feeling around 11 a.m., once you've had a chance to wake up and start the day. If you're still really tired, then you should probably get to bed a bit earlier the next night!

DREAMS AND NIGHTMARES

Have you ever woken up after a really vivid dream — maybe something zany and super-fun, or even something scary — and found yourself wondering, *Where on earth did that come from?!* Well, it's all to do with your brain sorting out information.

When we sleep, we go through two main stages or types of sleep: rapid eye movement (REM) sleep and non-REM sleep. We dream during REM sleep, and you can tell if someone is in this stage because you'll see their eyes flicking around under their eyelids as if they are

watching an action movie.
Your dog is also in REM
sleep if you see them
twitching about — they're
probably dreaming of
chasing rabbits or a ball!

During REM sleep your
brain is replaying
bits of what you
have experienced and
deciding what to store
as memories and what
to get rid of. These are your dreams.
But because your brain isn't doing it in order, instead
taking tiny pieces of events from throughout your day
and jumbling them up, the results can be very strange!
It's like putting the pieces of different jigsaws together
— the finished picture probably won't resemble any of
the original jigsaws. We're also processing our emotions
during this time, so getting enough sleep helps us to
control our feelings better when we are awake.

If there is something you're worried about, you may
end up dreaming about it because your brain is trying
to work it out. So if there is a particularly difficult
question you are stuck on for your homework, try
working on it just before you go to bed and then put it

out of your mind. When you wake up in the morning, you might find it a bit easier. Thank your amazing brain!

SLEEPWALKING

When we sleep, our brains deactivate our bodies so that we don't move around very much during our dreams. Otherwise that could be pretty dangerous. Imagine dreaming about being an Olympic athlete and trying to do a high jump in your bed!

However, some people find that their body wakes up while the brain remains asleep, so they end up doing things as if they were awake. We call this sleepwalking. People who sleepwalk have no control over their actions and may not even remember doing any of them afterwards! Some people have ended up getting out of bed and getting ready for work — even leaving the house.

Sleepwalking is much more common in kids than grown-ups. Luckily it isn't harmful and most children grow out of it by the time they are teenagers. Often it's just because you're not getting enough sleep and it's a sign you need to go to bed sooner. If it's really bad, then you may need to see a sleep specialist about it.

THREE STEPS TO BETTER SLEEP

All of us will struggle to sleep properly at some point. Usually it's because we've got into some bad habits at bedtime. If you're going through a rough patch, try my sleep-saving tips:

1) **POWER-DOWN HOUR** — have a bedtime routine for an hour at the end of every day which involves going to bed at a similar time each night, winding down with something like a bath and a book, and trying not to use any electronic devices. TVs, tablets and phones give off a certain kind of light from their screens which keep our brains stimulated, so it's harder for us to feel sleepy.

2) **SNUGGLE TO SLEEP** — try to make your bedroom as sleep-friendly as possible by keeping it calm, quiet, comfortable, dry and dark. You can use a night light (or keep the corridor light on outside your room) if you don't like total darkness.

3) **HAPPY THOUGHTS** — relaxing your mind and thinking about good things that have happened during the day, rather than things that are worrying you, will help you drift off. You could even think about things that you are looking forward to tomorrow or later in the week. We'll talk more about dealing with worries later in this chapter.

If you are still finding it really difficult to get to sleep each night even after you've tried the above, speak to a grown-up. You might need to see a doctor to get some help.

LET'S TALK MENTAL HEALTH

Remember, mental health is the term we use to describe how well your mind is working. So we're talking about what you're feeling and how you're coping with your thoughts and emotions.

Have you ever wondered where your feelings come from? I don't mean feeling annoyed at your little sister because she drew all over your favourite book (not this one, I hope!). What about feelings like happiness or fear?

Once upon a time, people used to think that your feelings came from your heart (a bit like the ancient Egyptians we mentioned at the start of the book). Sometimes people still talk about this. You've heard the phrase 'a broken heart', where you feel really sad, right?

But thanks to science, we know that the heart is focused on pumping blood around the body, and feelings come from your brain. There is a particular part of your brain that deals with these things. It's called the amygdala. This is the bit that is in charge of our emotions.

The amygdala receives messages from all the other parts of the brain that deal with your senses (such as touch, sight, smell, hearing). It also sends messages to other areas. So if you see something frightening, like a snake, the amygdala gets messages from your eyes about what it is seeing and tells the rest of your brain to be scared. If it's something you might need to remember for the future, then your amygdala will create a memory of the event and 'tag' on the emotion too. In this case you'll remember to feel scared the next time you see a snake. A similar thing happens for pleasant experiences too — like seeing your friends instead of a snake!

Feelings can be positive or negative. Positive feelings make you feel good. These include things like happiness, joy, love, kindness, friendship and excitement. All that lovely stuff! Negative ones make you feel less good. These include anger, sadness, hate, worry and fear.

DEALING WITH DIFFICULT FEELINGS

There will be times when you feel amazing. Like
that time you opened a box of cereal and there were
T W O free toys inside instead of one. And there
will be times when you don't feel so great. Like when
you've fallen out with a friend or you've lost your PE
kit and have to tell your mum.

It's important to remember that all of these different
feelings are normal. We don't feel just one thing all the
time and we don't feel the same every day. It's part of
being human! Do you remember the last time you felt
sad? Or angry? It will have felt pretty horrible at the
time, but it didn't last for ever, did it?

That's the thing about difficult feelings — they usually
get better. So it's OK not to be OK sometimes. It's OK
to feel sad and to cry. Sometimes it helps! And usually
you'll end up feeling absolutely fine afterwards. And
sometimes, feeling the not-so-good stuff makes us
appreciate the nice feelings more. But that doesn't
mean we can't figure out ways to manage those difficult
feelings so they are easier to handle when they do
crop up.

WORRIES

It's super-normal to be worried now and again. If you find yourself feeling worried a lot, why not create a feelings journal? Here's how:

1) At the end of the day, write down anything that is worrying you on a page in a diary or journal. This helps to stop the worries just endlessly buzzing about your brain.

2) On the page next to it, write down things that have made you feel great that day too. This reminds you that there are good things that happen to you as well.

3) Show the journal to a grown-up you can trust and talk about your worries. They can help you deal with them and may be able to make you feel better. Always try to talk to someone about anything that is worrying you — it's much better than keeping your feelings bottled up!

FIGHTING YOUR FEARS

I remember being worried a lot as a kid. I was worried about doing well at school. I was worried about having friends. I was worried about being made to play rugby (which I really didn't like because I was the smallest one in the class). I was even worried that there was a giraffe living under my bed. OK, I might have made that last one up.

Facing your fears and worries is about being brave. Everyone can be brave if they have to — including you! Just remember that you and your brain can do so many awesome things that there is nothing you can't overcome if you put your mind to it.

Some people have a really bad fear of something and we call that a phobia. That's where you are really scared of something and it may stop you from doing certain things. There are hundreds of different types of phobia, but here are some examples. Some can even seem a bit funny — but they probably don't feel like that to the person experiencing them.

ARACHNOPHOBIA — fear of spiders
LINONOPHOBIA — fear of string
GLOBOPHOBIA — fear of balloons
OMPHALOPHOBIA — fear of belly buttons
TUROPHOBIA — fear of cheese

Luckily, if you have a phobia of something then you can overcome it. You could try the following:

1) Most phobias aren't actually going to hurt us — so just keep reminding yourself that the thing you're afraid of won't harm you. For example, some

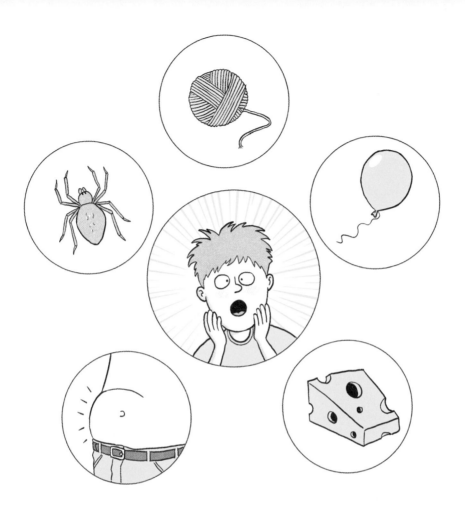

people hate blood tests because they are scared of needles. However, even though the needle feels sharp, it won't actually cause you any harm and will be gone in less than a minute!

2) Build yourself up slowly to face it. For instance, if you're scared of spiders, start by looking at pictures of them. Then try being in the same room as one. Then get closer. Then maybe move your hand closer to it before eventually letting it touch

you. Take your time, as this can be difficult. And remember that the spider is more scared of you than you are of it!

3) Tell those around you how you are feeling. That way they can look out for you in case you're overwhelmed, and it can help you feel a bit safer. So if you're scared of heights and you have to go to the top of a building, ask your friend to go with you.

If your phobia is really bad, you can get help from a specialist, like a psychologist.

POSITIVE POWER!

Now let's talk about the positive stuff. Thinking about positive things and showing positive emotions doesn't just make you feel better — it's actually good for you! Here's how:

1) **HAPPINESS** — did you know that when we are happy it helps our minds and bodies to relax? Happiness means we have less stress (that's another way of saying worry), and too much stress can be bad for us. So crack a joke every now and again and see if it gives your friends a giggle!

2) **KINDNESS** — when we are kind and do things for other people, it doesn't just help them. It helps our own minds too. Doing acts of kindness releases chemicals called hormones inside our brains that help us relax and feel good. So why not try to do something nice for someone else every single day?

3) **FRIENDSHIP** — having friendships and positive relationships with other people helps us to feel safe and gives us a sense of belonging. It also means we have someone to talk to when we're having a difficult time. In fact, just knowing that someone would be there for you if you needed them is really comforting. All of these things are good for our mental health. So why not make a new friend or speak to someone in class who you haven't spoken to before?

MENTAL HEALTH PROBLEMS

We all feel a range of emotions every day. Life is a rollercoaster and our thoughts and feelings can be too. Most of us are able to cope with these so that they don't stop us doing day-to-day things or cause more serious problems.

However, for some people their thoughts can become too much or they might feel like they can't manage them. This is when feelings might become a problem. Some examples of this are:

1)   Feeling sad or down a lot and not being able to enjoy the things you usually do.

2)   Feeling worried all of the time, which stops you from doing things.

3)   Feeling bad about food or not eating normally.

4)   Not being able to sleep properly.

5)   Feeling like you have to do certain things over and over to feel safe or calm.

6)   Feeling like you want to hurt yourself or someone else.

Mental health problems happen when our minds aren't working properly. This could be because of lots of reasons: sometimes people are just born a certain way, sometimes it's because of the way they have been looked after, sometimes it's because of the things they have seen or experienced. No matter what the reason, it's never that person's fault. It could happen to anyone at any age. The most important thing is to be able to spot when something isn't right and to ask for help.

There are different kinds of mental health difficulties too. You may even have heard grown-ups talking about them. Two of the most common ones are anxiety and depression.

ANXIETY

Let's start by explaining where anxiety comes from. When something stressful is happening to you, your body's natural defence mechanism kicks in. Your amygdala springs into action and your body produces certain hormones (such as adrenaline) that get it ready to either stand and fight or to run away to safety.

This is called the fight or flight response and it makes you feel anxious. This is something that humans have had for thousands of years and is there to keep you safe.

Feeling anxious sometimes is completely normal. We all get anxious in certain situations (like if you have an important test or audition). Usually it settles down quite quickly and you feel normal again. However, there are times when it gets out of control. It may happen for no reason, or be so bad that it stops you doing things, or might not go away very easily. This is what we mean when people talk about anxiety as a mental health condition, rather than a feeling we all get.

This anxiety can feel like intense worry, fear or panic that you can't control. You might get physical feelings too, such as a pounding heart or feeling sick or light-headed. Most people can learn to control and calm these feelings down themselves. However, some people need help from doctors or medicine.

If you find yourself getting anxious a lot, try the following useful tips to calm you down:

1) Tell yourself the feeling won't last for ever and you will feel better again.

2) Try to relax and stay as calm as you can. There are some relaxation exercises for you to try later in this chapter.

3) Don't avoid the things that make you anxious, as this can make it worse. Instead try to face them as best you can.

If you can't manage your anxiety feelings yourself, always speak to a grown-up. They might be able to help you or find you someone to speak to who can make things better.

DEPRESSION

Depression is another mental health problem that you may have heard people speak about. The best way to describe it is a feeling of sadness that doesn't go away, and it can last for weeks or even months. People with depression struggle to do and enjoy things that they usually would. They may also struggle to sleep.

It's normal to feel sad or down now and again. But that is different to depression because usually we can get over sad feelings and feel better again. People with depression can't just shake it off. They may even need to see someone like a doctor and get medicine for it.

My mum had depression when I was growing up. It was a really hard time for me and my brothers. It came out of nowhere and it took a long time for her to get it under control. At one point she had to stay in hospital for a short period of time to get special help. That's when I realised that what she had was a mental illness, and she needed treatment to get better. At the time it was quite scary but, looking back now, I know it was important for her to get the help she needed. It also reminds me that it can happen to anyone, which is why looking after your mental health is so important.

GETTING HELP

If you are finding it hard to cope with your thoughts and feelings, it's really important to speak to a grown-up about it. This could be someone in your family, a teacher at school or a health professional (like a doctor or nurse). Sometimes you may need to speak to someone who looks after people with mental health difficulties, such as a counsellor, psychologist, psychiatrist or a therapist. These people are there to help us manage our problems and feel better again.

The most important thing to do is to ask for help, and remember that you can feel better again!

CREATE YOUR CALM

One way that we can all look after our mental health is to teach ourselves how to calm unpleasant or unwanted thoughts and feelings down. It could be by doing something as simple as just taking a time-out and coming back when you feel better. Or you could try distracting yourself with something else to take your mind off it. So if you're worried about something, you could go for a walk, listen to some music or watch your favourite TV show. Or it could be taking yourself away to a place where you feel calm and safe until the emotion passes. I have a really comfy spot on my sofa by the window where I can just sit and stare at the world outside!

Here's a simple breathing exercise you can try if you're feeling stressed or anxious — we call it box breathing:

1) Sit in a comfortable place.

2) Close your eyes and just think about your breathing.

3) Breathe in slowly and count up to four as you do so in your head. At the same time raise your arm as if you were drawing one side of a box in the air.

4) Then hold your breath for a count of four. Move your arm across as if you were drawing the top of the box.

5) Then slowly breathe out for a count of four. Now you are moving your arm down, drawing the other side of the box.

6) Finally, hold your breath for a count of four and draw the bottom of the imaginary box.

7) You can keep repeating this until you feel calmer again. Then open your eyes!

It takes a bit of practice, but you'll soon get the hang of it!

Something else that I've found really helpful is mindfulness. You may already have learned about this at school. Mindfulness is a type of meditation which helps to calm your mind down. It involves concentrating on what you are feeling and experiencing right now. I find it super-useful when I just need to feel a bit more relaxed or think more clearly.

There are different types of mindfulness exercises you can do. Here's a really easy one:

1)   Sit somewhere comfortable and quiet. Close your eyes.

2)   Try to empty your mind and just concentrate on what your body is feeling.

3)   Starting with your feet, tense your toes for a couple of seconds and then let them completely relax.

4)   Then work your way up your body, starting from your feet, tensing each body part and then relaxing it.

5) Finally you should end up at your eyes. Screw them up really tight for a couple of seconds and then completely let go.

6) Your whole body should feel completely relaxed now ... and you've just spent a short time thinking of nothing but what your body is feeling. So just sit and enjoy it for a bit!

Here's another exercise to try that's even more focused on your breathing.

1) Sit somewhere comfortable and quiet. Close your eyes.

2) Try to empty your mind. If other thoughts come into your head, that's fine. Just let them pass. I imagine them like passing clouds that I am watching from afar.

3) Try to focus just on your breathing.

4) Let the air you are breathing come in to your body through your nose, fill up your lungs and then go out again through your mouth. You don't have to breathe at any particular speed, just whatever is comfortable for you.

5) Some people like to picture their breath as a different colour coming in and going out. I imagine it as a warm golden glow when it comes

in and then a cool blue as it goes out.
Whatever trick you use, just keep thinking
about your breathing.

6) Do this for a few minutes. If your mind wanders
don't worry, just bring it back to thinking about
your breathing again.

7) You should start to feel calmer already!

If you keep practising mindfulness, not only does it help
you to feel more relaxed, but you might notice that
you can concentrate on things better in general too. It
doesn't always work for everyone, but it's worth a try!

YOU DO YOU

Remember: we all have good days and not-so-good
days. We all feel a range of different emotions —
some amazing ones and some not so nice. All of this is
normal. Your brain is designed to deal with it all, but
sometimes each of us needs a little help.

What you are feeling or going through doesn't have to
decide who you are. You are capable of so much more
and there is so much you can do in the world. Right
now, you're just learning how to be your best, so don't
worry if you haven't got it all worked out straight away.

HARNESS YOUR BRAIN POWER!

There you go! You're now a — puts on special deep voice — Proper Brain Expert! I'm being serious. Now that you've come to the end of this book, you know so much more than when you started.

You've learned how we found out what the brain does and about all of the amazing people that made those discoveries. You now know what your brain is made of, how it's all put together and how it works as part of your nervous system. You've discovered what makes **YOUR** brain so special and unique. You also have some brilliant brain-training exercises you can try, as well as some great tips to look after your mental health.

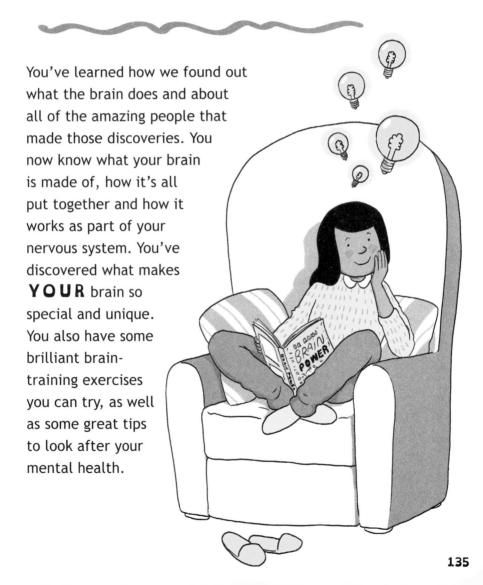

All so that you can get the most out of every day while keeping your brain and mind in top condition.

By reading this book you've activated millions of neurons in your nervous system. You've made many more synapse connections. Your brain has gathered new information and sorted it all out. Some of it has been stored in your memory banks to use in the future. On top of that, your mind has expanded and you will have a better understanding of and control over your feelings too. Remember that quote from René Descartes? I think, therefore I am ... I think you should add the word **AMAZING** on to the end of that.

I THINK THEREFORE I AM AMAZING!

QUIZ ANSWERS ...

Oh, I almost forgot! Remember that little quiz at the start of the book? You will have picked up the answers as you read each chapter, but here's a reminder ...

1)   Your brain is mainly made of water.

TRUE! Your brain is about three-quarters water. That's why it's important to drink enough fluid for it to work properly.

2)   Messages to or from your brain travel at 100 kilometres per hour.

FALSE! Electrical messages are carried around the body by your neurons and travel at speeds of around 400 kilometres per hour — that's a lot faster than your family's car.

3)   The animal with the biggest brain is the elephant.

FALSE! It's actually the sperm whale which has the biggest brain out of all animals. But their brains aren't very well developed, which is why they aren't as clever as humans.

4)   Sleep is important because it's when your brain makes memories.

T R U E! Sleep is when your brain organises itself, replenishes and recovers. It's when it decides what to keep as memories too.

5)   The left side of your brain controls the right side of your body (and vice versa).

T R U E! Your central nervous system crosses over so that the left side of your brain senses and controls the right (and vice versa).

If you didn't get them all right the first time, now you know! Your brain is already better than before!

EVERY BRAIN
IS BRILLIANT!

We all feel like our brains aren't
doing everything we need them to
sometimes. But remember: your brain
is the result of hundreds of thousands
of years of evolution. There is nothing
in the world quite like it. And there
is nothing in the world quite like you.
I want you to always remember that —
especially on days when you feel like
you're not able to do your best. You
have as many nerve cells in your
brain as there are stars in the sky.
It's like you have a whole galaxy inside your head! And
just like space is huge and the possibilities are endless,
so is your potential and the things that you could do.

No matter what anyone else says, you and I both know
that you have the ability to do anything if you put your
mind to it. We all have different strengths we can play
to. Everyone has something that they are especially
good at, so once you find your talent, make the most of
it. That could be dance or drama, it could be sport, it
could be science, or it could be writing and poetry. Or,
like me when I was growing up, it could be art!

We also all have a choice in what we do. Thanks to neuroplasticity, we can improve at the things we choose to spend time practising and working hard on. So if you love to do something — even if you're not very good at it — then keep going! You'll definitely get better over time but, even more important than that, you'll be having **FUN**.

EMBRACE AND CELEBRATE YOU!

Your brain is also responsible for you being who you are. So making the absolute most of it means embracing and celebrating **YOU** too!

As you now know, even though our brains look fairly similar, we are all unique. That's because we work in slightly different ways, we have different minds and we've had different experiences growing up. And those differences are what make us interesting. It's what helps us to stand out from the crowd.

When I was growing up, I was so shy that the last thing I wanted to do was stand out. Looking back on that time now, I wish I had just been brave enough to be me. First, I would have been so much happier. And secondly, it would have meant that I could have done so many

more things that I enjoyed —
like singing! Turns out this
is something I am quite
good at!

Whoever you are
and whatever
you like, you
have the
potential
to be
awesome.
And that starts
with believing in
yourself, being brave
and trying to be the
best version of you.
We all have things
that we find difficult,
but you can still be
great in spite of
all that.

NEVER BE AFRAID TO ASK FOR HELP!

Many of us will struggle with our minds as we grow up too. I faced challenges with my mental health even when I was a kid. I didn't really have anyone to talk to about it when I was younger. But now I know it's so important to speak to someone when you're struggling.

When times are tough, make sure you don't just keep it to yourself. Speak to those around you. Talk to a grown-up you can trust. That could be a member of your family, someone at school, a doctor or nurse, or someone like a counsellor.

There are some useful resources at the end of the book that you could use for information and help too. Whoever it is you speak to, never feel embarrassed or ashamed to ask for help. We all go through difficult times and we all need help sometimes. And then you can feel better again!

NOW GO AND BE BRILLIANT!

This is the part where I let you go and explore who you are and how to be the best you can be. But before you go, let me give you one more piece of advice that I wish someone had given me. Whoever you are and whatever you enjoy or are good at, remember that you are the perfect version of you. You may not have discovered it all yet, but there is so much **AMAZING** inside you. Don't worry, you'll find it. And when you do, make the most of it. You are brilliant!

RESOURCES

NEUROSCIENCE FOR KIDS
http://faculty.washington.edu/chudler/neurok.html
A really fun and fact-filled resource for kids who want to learn more about the brain and nervous system. Created by scientists and students at the Centre for Neurotechnology in Seattle, USA, this site has lots of information as well as some really cool games and experiments to try.

KIDSHEALTH
https://kidshealth.org/en/kids/brain.html
Not only can you learn more about the brain and nervous system, but this site also gives you information about various parts of your body and keeping it healthy. Everything is nicely divided up into things for kids, teens and their parents so there's something for everyone. And they have a great section on health conditions if you wanted to find out something more specific.

FRONTIERS FOR YOUNG MINDS
https://kids.frontiersin.org
This is a scientific journal for kids — edited by kids! They take cutting-edge scientific research and information and make it easy to understand for young, curious minds. They cover everything from neuroscience to astronomy, health to mathematics. This is the site for young people who want to push themselves to see what they can learn and do!

BBC BITESIZE

https://www.bbc.co.uk/bitesize

Want some free and interactive learning resources? BBC
Bitesize has you covered. It's full of stuff for all ages across
the school curriculum — including info for teachers and
parents. This site is mainly for UK users, but is helpful
for anyone who wants good-quality educational material
and activities.

MENTALUP

https://www.mentalup.co/brain-games

This site has over one hundred brain-training exercises and
games for kids created by the UCL Institute of Education. They
can help improve attention, concentration, memory skills and
imagination. It does require a subscription, but you can use it
for free for seven days and they offer family plans too.

AUTISM EDUCATION TRUST

https://www.autismeducationtrust.org.uk/kids-zone/

For any kids who want to learn more about autism. There are
also some great resources for parents and teachers here too.

YOUNG MINDS

https://youngminds.org.uk

Young Minds is one of the biggest mental health charities for
kids and young people in the UK. You can find help on lots of
different mental well-being topics, and they also run a helpline
for parents and carers.

GLOSSARY

adrenaline: A hormone produced by your body when you are excited, angry or scared, which makes your heart beat faster and gives you a rush of energy.

ambidextrous: Being able to use both hands equally well, rather than being left- or right-handed.

amygdala: Part of the brain that is involved in experiencing emotions.

anaesthetic: Medicine used to stop you feeling pain, e.g. during surgery.

anatomy: The study of body parts of living things and how they fit together.

artificial intelligence: The ability of computers to do things that usually require human intelligence.

Braille: A reading and writing system for blind people, where the alphabet is represented by patterns of raised dots.

cells: The smallest unit of life — all living things are made up of cells.

concussion: A type of brain injury caused by hitting your head, which disturbs the electrical activity in your brain cells.

counsellor: A person whose job it is to give advice, e.g. on personal problems.

CT scanner: A computerised or computed tomography scanner, which uses X-rays to make an image of the inside of your body.

embryo: One of the names given to a baby inside the womb when it is still in the early stages of development.

entomologist: A type of scientist who studies insects.

fight or flight: The response that your body has to something that seems scary or stressful — it releases hormones such as adrenaline and makes you feel anxious.

fMRI scan: A functional magnetic resonance imaging scan, which is a type of scan that doctors can do to see which part of your brain is active at any given time.

Frankenstein: A fictional book about a scientist called Victor Frankenstein, who tries to put different body parts together to create a living man.

growth hormone: A hormone produced by your body that helps it to grow and repair itself.

hormones: Chemicals produced by the body that are important in things such as growth and puberty.

kinaesthetic: To do with the position and movement of your body.

melatonin: A hormone produced by your body to help you sleep.

mental health: A term used to describe the health or well-being of the mind.

MRI scanner: A magnetic resonance imaging scanner, which uses radio waves and magnetic fields to make an image of the inside of your body.

mummify: A process the ancient Egyptians used to preserve someone's body after they died.

muscle memory: The ability to carry out an action without thinking about it because you've repeated it so many times.

nerves: Fibres in your body, like cables or wires, that carry electrical signals to or from your brain — they make up your nervous system.

neural tube: A structure inside an embryo that develops and grows into the brain, spinal cord and nervous system.

neurodiversity: A term referring to the differences between human brains and how they work.

neurologist: Doctors who look after people with brain or nervous system problems.

neuron: Also known as a nerve cell — a type of cell that carries electrical signals and forms part of the brain or nervous system.

neuroplasticity: The brain's ability to form new connections and reorganise itself, e.g. to learn or to recover after a brain injury.

neuroscientist: A type of scientist who studies the brain and nervous system.

neurosurgeon: A doctor who performs surgery on the brain and nervous system, also called a brain surgeon.

papyrus: A paper-like material that was used to write on in ancient times.

PET scan: A positron emission tomography scan, which doctors use to see what is happening in different parts of the body.

phobia: An extreme fear of something.

physiologist: A type of scientist who studies how living creatures and their bodies work.

psychiatrist: A type of doctor who looks after people with mental health difficulties.

psychologist: An expert on the human mind and behaviour, who may look after people with mental health difficulties.

reflex arc: A process in the nervous system that allows you to have a fast reaction without even thinking about it, e.g. in response to something painful or dangerous.

REM sleep: Rapid eye movement sleep — a type of sleep during which you have dreams.

seizure: Sudden, disorganised electrical activity in the brain that happens with some illnesses or disorders, such as epilepsy.

spinal cord: The bundle of nerves running from the base of your brain down your back — part of your central nervous system.

synapses: The connections neurons make with each other, e.g. when you learn something.

therapist: A professional who helps people with their mental health.

transplant: An operation that involves moving a body part to another body, or to a different part of the body.

womb: The place inside a woman's body where a baby grows before it is born.

zoologist: A type of scientist who studies or is an expert on animals.

INDEX

ACKNOWLEDGEMENTS

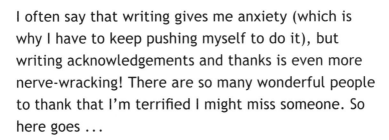

I often say that writing gives me anxiety (which is why I have to keep pushing myself to do it), but writing acknowledgements and thanks is even more nerve-wracking! There are so many wonderful people to thank that I'm terrified I might miss someone. So here goes ...

Thanks first of all to Liza Wilde, Victoria Walsh and the awesome team at Hachette. You've done it again! You've managed to take all the various ideas in my brain and order them into something I hope lots of little ones will enjoy and find helpful for years to come. Thanks also to our brilliant illustrator, David O'Connell, who has done an incredible job bringing the words to life again. Your work is simply beautiful.

Thanks to my fantastic management team who look after and over me every step of the way: Craig Latto, KT Forster and Jamie Brenner. Your help and guidance have been invaluable and I couldn't do this without you!

Thanks as always to my dear friends and family who continue to inspire me in everything I do. Each and every one of you has taught me something that has contributed to the content of this book. For that I am forever grateful.

And last, but not least, my most heartfelt thanks to Kay, Catrin and Tara, who all shared their knowledge and experience of neurodiversity. Your words will help so many children and young people.

There you go. I hope I haven't missed anyone out — if I have, just blame my brain!

Oh, I knew I would forget something ... thank YOU, our readers, for giving this book a chance. I hope you love it and share it with others. Let's help each other discover and celebrate everything we are. The world will be a better place for it.

Lots of love,

R x